CW01455682

SOUL STORY

HOW TO TELL STORIES THAT CALL IN YOUR SOUL TRIBE

CATE BUTLER ROSS

THE
LUMINOUS
PRESS

SOUL STORY

Copyright © 2023 Cate Butler Ross

Published by **The Luminous Press, 2023**

London, The United Kingdom

No parts of this publication may be reproduced, stored in a retrieval system, or transmitted in any form or by any means, electronic, mechanical, photocopying, recording, or otherwise, without the prior written permission of the copyright owner.

This book is sold subject to the condition that it shall not, by way of trade or otherwise, be lent, resold, hired out, or otherwise circulated without the publisher's prior consent in any form of binding or cover other than that in which it is published and without a similar condition including this condition being imposed on the subsequent purchaser. Under no circumstances may any part of this book be photocopied for resale.

Cover Art: Wild Honey Design

❀ Created with Vellum

This is for the change-makers; the dream-chasers
and the troublemakers;
this is for the light-weavers, the healers and the visionaries.
Because your stories hold the magic…

CONTENTS

PART ONE
AWAKEN THE STORYTELLER

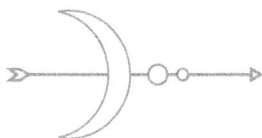

INTRODUCTION

WORDS THAT FEEL GOOD

YOU'RE A VISIONARY, a creative, an entrepreneur driven by a purpose; someone who loves to create, communicate and connect. You know you have something valuable to share – a mission or a worldview – and you dream of that message rippling across the globe like one big Mexican wave.

This is your soul work. It doesn't matter if you're a healer; coach; artist; activist; or teacher; whether your work is a private passion; or if it also happens to be the way you pay your bills – you have a calling to communicate what you've learnt; what you think; what you know; what you create; and what you believe. To do that, you need to position yourself as a leader – someone who not only *serves* but also *inspires*; someone who not only *connects* and *resonates*, but also *guides*. And to do *that*, you need to reach more people with your work.

Of course, connecting with more people and letting them know what you can do for them is what marketing is for. But when you're heart-centred and anti-hustle, this can feel hard. All those old-school and 'Bro' marketing techniques that everyone seems to be using these days, just don't feel good to you. They don't sit right.

The thing is, you don't want to move your audience to action
with (sometimes questionable) *tactics*,
you want to *really move them, heart and soul.*

And, while the more people you reach the better, it's not really about the numbers for you either. It's about calling in *your soul tribe*; the ones who accept you for who you are; the ones whose lives can be changed by what you have to say – and that might be 200 people or it may be two million.

Back in 2019, that's exactly how I was feeling. I'd been teaching entrepreneurs how to write content for just over a year – as an ex-magazine journalist, I'd written tens, maybe even hundreds of feature stories about small businesses, so when I looked to start my own business, supporting entrepreneurs was something that felt good to me, as did the idea of content marketing. The hard sell and the hustle was so against my nature, but content was all about attraction; offering value; creating connection, and always about giving more to your audience than you ever asked for in return – and that I could roll with.

All those 'Shoulds'…

I decided to market to heart-centred women entrepreneurs, because as something of a sensitive soul, I felt that was who 'I got' and who 'got me.' I started to grow an audience, I signed clients and students, and alongside classic copywriting skills, I started to teach what I now call *Content with a Heartbeat*, which is all about creating content that gets results, but also feels genuine and good. But after 18 months or so, just as I was beginning to find my feet in the online world, I started to feel like I'd totally lost my own way. I'd joined a mastermind, bought courses, had private coaching and mentorship, read tons of books and listened to hundreds of podcasts, but the more I became immersed in the online world, the more I was told what *'I should'* be doing. And creating great content wasn't enough.

I should be showing up every day; I should be niching and designing my whole brand around one ideal customer; I should be doing launches; I should be doing ads; I should be doing videos, and be on this platform and that platform; I should be doing intensive email marketing campaigns (and sending several emails out in quick succession on the day cart closes); I should be using scarcity, and, and, and...

And because I'm a good student and really wanted my business to work, I did all of it. Some of it didn't work, but I also had some real successes and celebrations, and from the very first programme I ever sold, I never once created anything that didn't sell anything at all. The problem for me though was it felt a lot like hustle, and it didn't feel good.

In March 2019, I got ill, and after several blood tests the doctor told me I was suffering from exhaustion. I'd burnt myself out and I still hadn't built the business or creative life I craved. I wrote in my journal, *'I want to feel passionate and fully expressed in my life and business. I want to be creative and free and true.'* I didn't feel any of those things. The truth was I didn't want to build my whole brand around a rigid avatar and offering; and while I knew I'd sometimes have to do things that went beyond my comfort zone, I never wanted to do anything that went against my nature. And I didn't want to put myself in a box, when, quite frankly, I'm a fluid, unpredictable, cyclical woman with many passions and interests and loves. I felt like all these rules were squashing me down, making me wrong, holding me back. I didn't really know what the answer was...

...AND THEN ONE DAY I SHARED A STORY.

I can't follow that with the words, *'and then my life changed completely.'* Because although things have changed since then, it wasn't really a dramatic change that happened overnight, but a gradual one. One day I told an honest story about my real life, and the handful of comments and emails that story attracted from my then fairly quiet subscriber list, encouraged me to write another, and another after that, until storytelling became the standard way for me to communicate.

I received more emails, more connections, and beautiful relationships were built within my audience. I felt connected, creative, and like all that showing up was actually making a difference in some small way to the people who read my words, and this motivated me to share more. And suddenly, somewhere along the way, through telling stories, I felt all those things I'd longed to feel; seen, passionate, fully expressed, creative and free.

This book is not an alternative to traditional marketing; it's not your Get Out of Jail Free Card to never have to list build or do PR or think about strategy. The basic pillars of marketing are and always will be an important part of business. This book won't tell you how to make seven figures or how to grow your audience to 10K either, although if you want to do those things what you're going to learn will no doubt be a powerful tool. What I hope this book will show you is that there is a different way to show up and share your message with the world; a simpler way, that with the right encouragement and a little know-how, you may find comes very naturally to you; a gentler way, that's both heart-led and powerful.

And that way starts with a story; your *soul story.*

Cate,
June 2022

BEFORE WE BEGIN

BONUS RESOURCES

ONCE YOU'VE READ this book, I want you to be a storyteller. I don't want you to just know the theory; I want you to be actually calling in your soul tribe through courageous and impactful storytelling – whether that's on online, on stage or in print.

That's why to help you implement what you're about to learn, I've made all of the formulas and frameworks you'll find inside this book (plus my Story-Storming Playbook that helps you unearth your story goldmine), available as free PDF downloads.

So, before you forget, go ahead and download your bonus materials now at www.theluminous.media/bonus/

CHAPTER 1

WHY STORY?

YOUR AUDIENCE WANTS REAL. They crave genuine connection. They don't want to be bamboozled or feel like they've been knocked around by psych 101. They want you, your message, your guidance, your truth, and the easiest way to give that to them is through storytelling.

Story moves; story captivates; story impacts;
and (remembering it's OK to earn money from your gifts), story sells.

But how do you use story in your communications in a way that will get your *soul tribe* to listen? How do you actually tell a good story? Or recognise you have a story to tell in the first place? Well, that's what this book is about, and the first thing to understand is that *your soul story* is an ever-filling cup; there's no scarcity here and there's always more where that came from.

You don't just have 'A Story,' you have 'Stories'

Your *Soul Story* isn't just one story either. Yes there's 'your story', in other words a curated series of events that got you to wherever you are right now. If you're called to get visible in this world, working out what that story is makes it a lot easier to do things such as:

1. Be remembered for the right reasons at networking events, because you've shown up as more than just your job title.
2. Explain to a potential client what makes you different to the other guys.
3. Share your 'why?' with the world, without sounding like a robot who swallowed a Thesaurus.

Everyone has a story. Even if you're not really sure what it is yet, you do. If you don't know what it is, the exercises in this book will help you to work it out. But remember, Soul Story is also about *your stories*. And your stories are a goldmine; one of the most colourful, original and creative assets you own. *Your stories* are what make you unique, and you have a ton of them; stories that will get you remembered for who you are and what you stand for; stories that can inspire; stories that can serve; and stories that can connect. Inside this book, you're going to learn how to unearth them all, and how to spot the new ones that you're constantly creating, which, by the way, is such an important skill because storytelling isn't one size fits all. It's not about repeating an anecdote that someone (or many someones) have already told.

LESSON
Soul Story is about framing your message
with a story only you can tell

Sharing a story only you can tell may feel intimidating, scary or even impossible right now. But as I'll remind you more than once, even if your story doesn't seem big enough, glamorous enough or different enough, the best story you can tell is *always* the true one.

Leaders tell stories on purpose

It's true, storytelling does come more easily to some people than others, but storytelling isn't pot-luck either, it's a craft. And it's also a craft that you've been using and absorbing since you were tiny. That's why storytelling is something you can learn to do on purpose, and once you can do that you can do things like:

1. Choose the right story for the right moment.
2. Start your story in the right place (which isn't necessarily the beginning).
3. Know what to tell them next and how to leave them wanting more.

That's why the storyteller really can be the most powerful person in the room – I didn't coin that, of course, Apple founder, Steve Jobs did (we'll hear more from him later on). But the point is, when you're a storyteller, there's no more…

Whispering from the back row….
because from your first words all eyes (and ears) are on you.
Wondering whether people liked your email, blog or talk….
because they're already contacting you to tell you how it made them think or feel
Forgettable cookie-cutter social media posts….
because you've framed your message with a story that no-one else can tell.

Sharing your stories is an act of courage

Storytelling isn't just about learning the craft though, because one of the first things you need to start telling your own stories is courage. There's no doubt about it, it takes guts to use your own failures and triumphs, challenges and heartbreaks to help, inspire and entertain others. So, before we launch into the technical side of things in Parts 2 and 3, we're going to talk about the mindset side of things too, because that is the key to becoming a more powerful storyteller. Good storytelling that comes from the heart is not just about the craft.

Take me as an example. I've taken writing seriously even when I was not a serious writer. In fact, one summer holiday when I was about 9 or 10 years old, I even taught myself to touch-type on my Dad's Apple Mac so I could write my (rather inspired by the latest teen thriller) stories faster. In my 20s, I attended lectures and classes; took university courses; read book after book on craft; and when I graduated from journalism school, I spent more than 15 years writing stories for the UK's top glossy magazines. Yet, as you'll learn, when I started my own business and created my own platform, the last thing I actually was able to do was tell my Soul Story.

It didn't matter that I knew I had to let people in if I wanted to make a connection, because there were too many reasons (and funnily enough, stories) around why this was a very *bad idea.* And so all the experience in the world couldn't help me at that point. Unravelling those stories and sabotages, however, did. And that's why *Soul Story* isn't just about teaching you how to tell a story through a bunch of step-by-steps and formulas.

Soul Story is also about conscious communication

I also talk about responsible storytelling; conscious storytelling. Because while I'm sure everyone reading this will

always have the best intentions when sharing a story, uncon-
scious communication is incredibly easy to slip into and can
have some unintended consequences. So we'll be diving
deeper into that, so you can make sure every story you tell is
consciously shared.

Craft and Soul

Finally, in Part 3, we will cover craft, and all the things
you need to know to get started with telling great stories. But
before you do any of that, you need to find the courage to
share what's truly on your heart, because all the formulas and
techniques and bells and whistles, can't make up for a lack of
soul.

Telling stories helps you grow

Let's be frank. Sometimes, sharing your true story, un-
gilded and unfiltered, can feel like giving away pieces of your
soul and metaphorically stripping yourself naked before an
unknown and unseen audience. Sounds fun, doesn't it? But
actually, communicating through story can also be a hugely
cathartic, insightful, yes, at times uncomfortable, but ultimately liberating experience too. Growing as a storyteller
takes self-awareness and self-compassion, and it can teach
you so much about yourself. Time and again I've found that
when I stop hiding on the page, I stop hiding in my life.

Stories are like avocados

Of course, I want to help you tell your story, but only
when it's ripe and ready to go. Just because something
happened and other people might be interested in that occur-
rence, doesn't mean you have to talk about it. You should
never force yourself to tell a story, and while we must be

mindful about sabotages (more on those in a sec), you'll usually know if your story is ready to tell, because it will just sort of slip out of its skin like a perfectly ripe avocado (unlike avocados, however, your story probably doesn't have a tiny window of deliciousness before it gets all mushy and disappointing).

When I told my husband I was writing this book to help people share more stories about their lives, he said (like the typical, no-nonsense Northern Irishman he is), *'Too many people share too much about their lives already.'* True, there is certainly no shortage of people willing to overshare in a Facebook post, but I'm not talking to those people. I'm talking to you; and I trust that you're somebody who has stories that will help and heal, but for some reason you haven't shared them yet. *Why is that, by the way…?*

Why aren't you telling your stories?

It might be through a lack of knowledge of where to start with storytelling; again, don't worry, this book's got you covered. Or it might be because you're full of doubt.

We're so good at doubting ourselves, aren't we? Well, I invite you to doubt those doubts. Because some of the stories I now share on my blog, in my podcast, with my email list, in my courses, and even inside this book, I'd never have dreamed of telling two years ago, either because they were too personal, or because I just didn't think they were relevant to what I do. As you'll learn, a good storyteller finds inspiration everywhere, and is constantly evolving, finding gold in old stories, and creating new ones.

What if your stories aren't enough?

Maybe you're thinking this book isn't for you after all. It's for people with bigger lives, bigger dreams, bigger achievements, bigger missions. No. I wrote this book for you. I want you to share your stories, because there's someone out there who needs to hear them. Trust me, I'm a journalist.

Well, I was. Back in my 20s and 30s, working as a features writer on magazines including *Country Living Magazine* and *Woman and Home*, I met a lot of incredible people and heard a lot of incredible stories. There were actors, Olympians, politicians, thought-leaders. I had lunch at television cook Mary Berry's house (she made me roast lamb and lavender shortbread and gave me a tour of her garden); I've made a scented candle with Jo Malone in her perfume studio while she shared her classic story of rags to riches; and I met the late *'Carry On'* actress Barbara Windsor in the Soho Hotel, who told me about her lifetime in show business over a bottle of Prosecco. During conversations like these I was often starstruck and had many a goosebump moment, but no more than I ever did with the hundreds of stories I heard from everyday people just like you and me.

Entrepreneurs; activists; artists; scientists; artisans; parents; teachers; healers; creatives; charity workers; community leaders; the list goes on. And all of them (even the beardy fungus expert a cereal company randomly asked me to write a blog about) had a story worth telling. It's just that sometimes you need a guide to help you work out things such as:

What is my story?
Who wants to hear it?
How can I tell it in a way so people will listen?

This book is your guide.

Everyone has a platform, but not everyone has a voice.
In my 20s, I worked on the features team of *Country Living*

Magazine, and we used to get at least one huge hessian sack of mail that was big enough to squash an intern, every single day. Those bags were stuffed with letters from people hoping we'd give a platform to their business or cause by telling their story in our magazine. Those were the days when the internet was a bit of a novelty that would *'never replace print journalism'* (ha-ha), so the only real platforms out there, were those that belonged to the legacy media. That's why small businesses and artisans were so keen for us to share their stories, because they knew it could be a total game-changer. So when I pitched stories to my editor about nurses who started their own cupcake businesses, or bereaved parents who'd created amazing charities, I became those people's advocate; and if I went on to write a feature about them, I became the steward of their story. I loved that about my job, because I felt like I was making a difference to their small business or raising awareness for an important mission or cause. The problem was, there were thousands of people like that out there, and I couldn't help them all.

If only they could be their own advocates. If only they didn't have to rely on gatekeepers like journalists and editors and agents and publishers, to decide if their story was worth sharing. If only they could be the stewards of their own stories and tell them with courage and confidence. If only they had their own platforms where they could connect with their people whenever they liked; and could write their own books and professionally publish them themselves.

Imagine a world like that…

Becoming a storyteller gives you the key

These days anyone reading this book can have all those things I've just mentioned above. You probably already have your own platform, whether it's through social media or your own website, and if you want to write a book down the line, being an indie author can be a strategic and tide-turning decision. But right now, maybe you're struggling to create connection or to effectively communicate your message. If that's the case, storytelling will help you. Why did all those businesses want to get into the features section of *Country Living Magazine and Woman* and *Home*? Because that was where we told stories, and telling your story is one of the most powerful pieces of PR.

When you're able to tell your own stories, you no longer need a journalist to help you unpick your past, or a communications expert to tell you what to say; or even a crystal ball to figure out who you are and what you stand for. You no longer have to try to get noticed or push yourself forwards either – because when you're a storyteller, you become the most captivating voice in the room.

LESSON

Tell your own stories, be your own advocate

———

Give them a 'Once upon a time' and they're hard-wired to listen

A question I get asked a lot is *'So when should I use story?';* And the answer is quite simply, *all the time.* You can be using story when you're teaching, connecting, relationship-building; and not just in professional situations either, but all the ways you show up in this world, as a parent; a colleague; a friend; a community member.

STORY IS THE MOST POWERFUL WAY TO SHOW UP.

There are lots of reasons for this, but the main one is that as humans our brains are wired towards story. Stories are how we make sense of the world and situations. They are how we filter the millions of pieces of information our brain receives at any given moment, and organise it into something that makes sense. Story is a bridge that takes your audience from whatever pain, or struggle, or confusion, or apathy your audience is in when you find them, to that place of inspiration, or hope, or encouragement, that makes them feel ready to take the next step. That next step may be buying a product or service from you, but equally it may simply be making different choices in their lives, thinking more deeply about a topic, or feeling anew about a challenge or situation. A good story is a crucible; it changes people – how they think, how they feel, and how they act.

Story creates connection

If you're called to communicate with an audience for your work, your passion or your calling, here are a few scenarios for which storytelling can be a powerful connector.

- *You want to call in your Soul Tribe.*

Who are your Soul Tribe? Quite simply the ones who need to hear your message; the ones you don't have to pretend with or put a mask on for; the ones who need your knowledge, inspiration or help; the ones who love you *just as you are.* Your Soul Tribe want to hear and will be attracted to your personal stories.

- *You have valuable knowledge or expertise that you want to share.*

If you're anything like me, when you know or understand something that can change people's lives, you want to tell them. But one thing I've learnt is that no matter how passionate you are about something, telling someone about the concept or idea rarely gets them engaged or as excited as you are. That's because it's hard to connect with a concept emotionally; concepts are abstract, intangible, hard to relate to in real life. Frame your concept with the right story though, and what you're trying to say has more chance of landing.

- *You don't want important lessons to fall on deaf ears*

My grandparents and parents often talked in proverbs. *'A stitch in time saves nine", "That's the pot calling the kettle black,"* or *"Don't count your chickens...."* As a child, I'm not sure I always totally got what they were on about, but even as a grown up who understands what it all means, when I hear them now, they don't feel like wisdom, more like knee-jerk phrases one says in a particular situation. The truth is old proverbs and adages have often lost their power and potency through overuse, but the wisdom is still worth sharing. True leaders, therefore, frame their sage advice in original and fresh ways, and there's no more an original and fresh way than by using one of your own stories.

- *You want to deepen your relationship with your audience.*

Most of the content I follow on social media is from real people that I care about. The funny thing is, I haven't actually met most of them. I've rarely even had a chat with any of them in the comments of their posts, and yet I don't wait for them to pop up on my newsfeed – I go to their websites, I search for their profiles, because I want to know what's going on in their world, and what they're creating. That's because as well as offering me value, they've built a relationship with me, and they've done this by letting me into their lives through stories. If you want your audience to care about you, to be loyal and seek you out, tell them stories that let them in.

- *You want to grow your authority.*

Of course, you want to show you're the right person to help them, but no-one cares about your CV or what qualifications you've got. Instead, you can illustrate your expertise, your experience and your results, through the stories of what you've done.

- *You want to show the value you offer.*

Think of the times you've spontaneously donated to charity – is it usually because someone has presented you with a set of unassailable or sobering statistics that have moved you to action? Or is it usually because you've heard a story? For me, it's always the latter, and anyone in the UK who's sat and watched *Children in Need* or *Comic Relief* will know exactly what I mean. As a leader, part of your mission is to educate your audience and help them to see things differently. But nobody wants to be lectured all the time. Don't tell them, *show* them, with a story.

SUMMARY

WHY STORY?

- Your stories are the most original and valuable assets you own.
- The best leaders frame their message with a story only they can tell.
- Storytelling is about having the courage to speak your truth.
- Story creates connection and builds relationships.

———

CHAPTER 2
HOW YOUR STORY CAN CHANGE IT ALL

GREW UP ON STORIES. Yes, I was a huge bookworm, but that's not what I'm talking about. What I mean is that I was raised on the *spoken story*; old wives' tales, if you like; specifically the stories told to me by my relatives.

The funny thing is, the main storyteller in my life, my maternal grandmother, would probably never consider herself a storyteller at all. She was a Londoner; the daughter of a black cab driver; an evacuee who literally ran away from her billet back to the Blitz; the belle of the war-time West End dance halls; a housekeeper for ladies and gentleman; a grandmother with oodles of energy (not to mention an acid wit); but I doubt she ever once considered herself a storyteller. And yet that and making gravy, in my eyes, is quite possibly her greatest skill.

We're not talking fairytales here. My Nan, who is now 96, is far too grounded for all that. All the stories she told us when we were growing up actually happened, but that didn't stop them from being laced with magic, because she instinctively knew how to tell them. The stories my Nan told us were the stories of her life, and those told to her by her mother and grandmother about their lives. There were no great lessons or morals she was trying to push, and she didn't tell us what to think about those stories, she simply told us what she knew and what had happened as a way to entertain on boring Sunday afternoons when it was raining outside and there was only the football scores on the telly.

It turned out though, that intentionally or not, those stories changed me: they moulded me and helped me to see my life in an entirely different context. But most importantly, they taught me how powerful the tales of ordinary lives can be. That's probably why feature writing became my thing. I loved finding apparently ordinary people and uncovering the stories that made them extraordinary. I also loved how sharing those stories could have such a profound impact on everyone involved: on the reader, who is inspired, or suddenly sees something differently, or is able to move past a challenge that had been holding them back; and for the story-teller themselves, who perhaps finds sharing their story healing or cathartic, or is able to see themselves in a different light, or experiences a surge of interest in their work.

A story can save a life

We've talked about how human brains are wired for story and there's a reason for that. Stories told around the hearth about wolves and poison apples taught us valuable lessons about survival; stories told in coffee houses and in drawing rooms started revolutions; stories about everyday acts of courage made way for more just systems; and today, it's most likely that it is a story that influences many of your actions, from how and if you vote, to where you shop, or how you feel about a particular person or cause.

Big business understands this. That's why it uses stories to paint just the right picture about their values and their purpose through their advertising campaigns and PR, so that for some, buying from a massive conglomerate can feel just as safe and ethical as buying from the man down the road. In fact, in the last 100 years, they've become so good at this, that the stories told by the world's biggest brands, innovators and organisations, have changed the very way we as humans have lived our lives for thousands of years – sometimes for the better; arguably often for the worse.

They've even changed the way we think and feel (or perhaps don't). One of the reasons that's been able to happen is because we've evolved to pay attention to stories, because there was once a time when a tale about a mysterious stranger or a powerful cure might just have saved your life. It is not economics, politics or even geography that really shapes our world therefore; it's the stories we hear.

Claim your stories.

I *still* believe a story can save your life, or at the very least change your life in a profound way. I also believe that *you* have at least one story that can change someone else's life for the better. When you become a storyteller, you have the power to impact your little sphere of influence, and no matter how small that sphere is, it does have a ripple effect. Your primary goal may be to reach more people so you can make more money doing the work you love; but as a visionary, a change maker and a heart-centred storyteller, you are also changing the tone of the collective narrative. Let me explain.

Imagine if every heart-led human started to claim their stories and began sharing them with intention. The entire tone of the collective narrative would no longer be dominated by the interests of global organisations who benefit from us feeling fearful and not enough, but by the unique voices of conscious individuals, of real-life humans with real lived experiences. If that happened, the narrative of the world would no longer be engineered, but find its natural harmony again. Now that *would* change the world. And the amazing thing is, you don't even need everyone to do it. Critical mass theory suggests you just need 30% for the dominoes to start to fall. And all the stories we need to tell to make that happen, are already there inside each and every one of us.

The truth is magnetic

We're going to be talking about the ready-made stories you already have to tell in Chapter 5, and by the end of Part 2, you'll have pages of stories ready to share, which for the right people, will be magnetic. Right now you may find this hard to believe. But I've often wondered why I was so captivated by my Nan's stories. Why were they so magnetic for me? It's not like there were any fancy balls or knights in shining armour, or handsome princes, or dastardly villains such as in the books I loved to read. Although, actually, is that true? Of course, there were all those things in her stories, and you'll find there will be all those things in your stories, too. Because fairy tales are just avatars of universal truths, with archetypes and symbols that represent real people, real problems and real situations that we all face in our real lives; the nasty neighbour becomes the wicked witch; the wise primary school teacher becomes the guide; the boy next door becomes the hero. The reason my Nan's stories have stayed with me and will stay with me always, is because what I was really listening to was her truth; her heart song; her soul story. And that's why I don't want to just inspire you tell any old story, I want to inspire you to tell *your soul story* – your *soul stories*. Because that's what makes you magnetic.

SUMMARY
HOW YOUR STORY CAN CHANGE IT ALL

Stories shape the fabric of the world we live in; the stories we hear influence our actions, our feelings and our beliefs; stories change lives. That means that when you become a storyteller, you have the power to impact your little sphere of influence; and it doesn't matter how small that sphere is, your stories can create a ripple effect.

———

CHAPTER 3
LEADING FROM THE HEART
WITH STORYTELLING

MIXING THE PERSONAL with the professional can feel unnatural, particularly if you've become accustomed to thinking of your work as something that's separate to your private life. To be fair, if previously you've only ever worked for someone else or been doing a job that didn't exactly light you up, your work probably never felt connected to you personally at all. When you start to do work that's soul-driven however, it becomes nothing but personal, and the people you're hoping to reach *do* care who you really are behind the job title. This leads to questions such as:

Who should I show up as?
What should I reveal?
And most urgently,
What should I hide?

Many aspiring communicators and storytellers are hiding. Some of them are fully in the shadows, but others are hiding in plain sight. In the early days of my business, I had a toddler who was at nursery a couple of mornings a week, and a baby. I was constantly either cooking, changing nappies, trying to get a child to sleep, or cleaning Play-Doh and mashed potato off the floor. I was ambitious, but I also wanted to be a mummy, which meant I was squeezing my work into the cracks and never felt like a 'legitimate' leader or entrepreneur.

I joined memberships and networking groups for women in business, I followed other people in my niche; and everyone else's businesses seemed so shiny, so together, so perfect. Even though I knew most of what we see online is at worst misleading and always curated, I still felt that to be taken seriously I must be as shiny, consistent, polished and perfect as they were. I was also very resistant to being labelled a 'mumpreneur', which was funny because I seemed very happy to climb into every other box around. There are lots of problems that come from trying to fit into somebody else's mould, but a big one is that pretending to be something you're not is exhausting and counter-productive.

What are you scared they'll find out?

As an ex-journalist, creating consistent content was easy for me. What wasn't easy was stepping into a different persona every time I showed up, and editing out the parts of my life and personality I didn't think fitted with my brand. Something about that approach felt vaguely wrong, but I ignored my intuition because I was too afraid of being 'found out'.

I'm not quite sure what I thought they'd *find out* about me exactly. Perhaps that I only ran my business two days a week, which made it feel more like a very exhausting hobby; or the fact that balancing my work with motherhood was a constant source of guilt and strain. Interestingly, I definitely was very coy about the fact that I was a former magazine journalist – for some reason I felt this gave me less credibility than everybody else in my field, and I was afraid to own my authority. I was also totally in the spiritual closet back then. To think that one day I would ever talk about writing, storytelling and communication in terms of magic, energy and vibration, would have definitely felt like one of those dreams where I accidentally turn up to a party in my koala bear slippers and an old dressing gown.

Are you visible but vanilla?

In order to conceal all of these dirty little secrets, I hid behind being 'professional', or at least my version of it. Every time I created content or went live in my Facebook group, I stepped into the persona I thought my audience wanted me to be: I was *visible but vanilla*; never standing out from the crowd. If you're reading this and suspect that you may be hiding in plain sight, just like I was back then, here are a couple of my biggest telltale signs you may find familiar:

1. You're always the expert

You show up, share huge value, but don't reveal much of your personality, your story, or behind the scenes of your life, because it feels too awkward and a bit weird. You feel like you're pretending; like you're in a clingy dress and constantly holding your tummy in. How you long to just let it all hang out…

2. You're held back by perfectionism.

You can't share it, do it, promote it, talk about it, or put it into action, until it's perfect. You're a slave to whether you've got a professional-enough photo, a slick-enough logo, a fancy-enough sales page. You'd never dream of showing any cracks or vulnerability because that would undermine your authority; you're a bit formal, you do things by the book; you're afraid of getting it wrong.

Being visible but vanilla may feel safe, but there's always a trade off. In this case it's that nobody falls in love with you or your message. People want connection and they don't get that from facts, information, formulas or clever taglines. You can't fall in love with a textbook or cardboard cut-out. That's why the question you really should be asking is not *what should I hide?* But *how can I lead more from the heart?*

Lesson

You can be consistently visible and still be hiding in plain sight. If you're showing up, but attracting few meaningful connections, the chances are you're hiding

———

The only person you should be following

If you want to put yourself out there and feel comfortable in your own skin, most of us have to do the inner work. Luckily, I had inherited a love of self-help books from my Dad and was already a total personal development junkie, and so I threw myself into the inner work of showing up with gusto, and as a result, like that tight bud with no choice but to bloom that Anaïs Nin was banging on about, I eventually had a revelation. Here it is:

When it comes to how to show up, the only person you need to follow is yourself; the only place you need to look for inspiration is you; because anything else is out of alignment with who you are, and does not attract the people who like you just the way you are. Boom.

When you position yourself as the face of your brand, as a leader in your field, *you are your work and you are your brand.* I don't mean by that, you are one and the same; I believe that every business has its own energy that is separate to its creator. What I mean is, the things that happen in your life when you walk away from your desk or studio, are not things that need to be boxed up and hidden. As a soul-led creator, your whole life is what informs your work. That means allowing yourself to be all the things you are when you show up in the world, because your vibe really does attract your tribe.

The day I sat down to edit this chapter, I happened to watch a video from Tim Whild, a spiritual teacher that I follow. He said:

> *'We are not here to fight our corner anymore;*
> *we are here to lead with the light of our vibration.'*

Tim, of course, is not talking about storytelling, he's talking about spiritual alchemy, because that's his thing. But there are no coincidences, only synchronicities, and what I took from that was this:

We don't need to fight and hustle using more and more clever marketing techniques to be heard – those days are gone. Your people don't want to be coaxed, persuaded or cajoled. Which means all that's left is to let your vibe do the talking. And that means showing up and sharing what's on your heart.

Own Your Weird.

Being yourself can feel like a risk. We worry:

Will the real me appeal to the kind of person I'm trying to attract?
Will this bit of me turn them off?
Will they be offended by that?

We all curate how we show up in public to a certain extent, of course. Because while I'm all for fully owning your weird, it doesn't always work within the parameters of say, school-gate small talk. But your soul work isn't small talk. It matters deeply. So if you're hiding who you really are in how you're showing up in that world, before long it will only start to feel exhausting and inauthentic. Your vibe attracts your tribe, so you are the one who calls in your audience. Which means you can choose to call in people who love you just the way you are, by *being* just the way you are. Or you can carry on pretending. It's your choice.

When I decided to start telling more stories about my life, rightly or wrongly I didn't worry about what relevance it had to that fictional character that was my *Ideal Client Avatar.* I stopped caring and second guessing and just started to share. This is not what most business coaches or marketing experts would advise. But again, I'm not here to replace their advice, I'm here to invite you to be the fullest expression of you, because I know that's what makes a person magnetic. And after all, if you can't be totally yourself when you're doing your soul work, then you're still just working for somebody else.

Friends you haven't met yet…

So, if we don't need to fit in a box anymore, surely it follows that our audience doesn't have to either, right? In fact, the only thing that they really have to have in common is that they resonate with you and your ideas and want your solutions. This realisation for me, was extraordinarily freeing. Because it also meant I could pivot in my business and my offering without stressing about whether my audience would come with me or not. That's because they were attracted to me and my ideas and creations, and not the specific elevator pitch I was using in 2019. The ones who were attracted just by that elevator would fall away, and I'd send them off with love, relieved that I didn't have to worry about pleasing them anymore.

One of the best things about the creator economy (and if your work is about sharing your ideas or knowledge it's an economy that you're part of), is that it gives you full permission to climb out of the box. For me, climbing out of the box meant my life could become a workshop of inspiration, projects and ideas, which I could share with my audience as and when I wanted through content. Suddenly I could share my whole journey with them as though they were not my audience, but my pen pals! And this created a level of intimacy that I'd never had with my communications before.

I think this approach is summed up perfectly by one of my favourite entrepreneurs, Leonie Dawson, who also refuses to be put into a box, and yet consistently attracts loyal fans who just want to be in her orbit. She describes her audience as 'friends I haven't met yet.' I agree that is exactly how it should feel. And what do you do when you catch up with a friend? Well, you tell them stories from your life like it's the most natural thing in the world, because of course, it is.

SUMMARY

LEADING FROM THE HEART WITH STORYTELLING

- Stop trying to fit into someone else's mould – the only person you should follow is you.
- Your vibe attracts your tribe – share from the heart and trust your people will find you.
- If you want to create a real connection and rapport with your audience, talk to them as though they are friends you just haven't met yet

———

———

'I was told when I first pitched a book that was not about periods that there was too much "I" in the book. "No one wants your story Lisa; no-one wants women's stories. You just need to tell us what the things are and how we fix it." Everyone wanted a five-point plan, everyone wanted a self-help fix-it book. And I was like, "What do you mean 'no "I"'?' All I've ever wanted was women's stories, all I ever crave is women's stories." I want to know how it is for you. I want someone's stories to reflect back my truth so I can recognise myself in their story.'

LISA LISTER, AUTHOR; EPISODE 40, THE CONTENT DOWNLOAD PODCAST

———

CHAPTER 4

STOP HIDING & START SHINING YOUR LIGHT

T HERE'S A SIXTH SENSE for when someone isn't being entirely true. Perhaps they feel hard to connect with or something just feels a bit false – a bit off. We all know what that feels like to pick up on, but as storytellers, leaders and communicators, we really don't want someone to have that feeling about us.

Working as a features writer I was well-practised in detecting when there was something left unsaid, and because it was my job to uncover and pursue the best story I could find, that meant digging deeper and asking the right questions, until whatever was niggling me made sense. However, there were a few occasions when I would start to ask questions about something and then stop, even though I knew that later I might be pulled up by my editors for doing so.

Perhaps I wasn't being a good journalist, but I did this because I don't believe in the idea of doing anything for a good story, not if it meant making someone feel vulnerable against their will. So, if I sensed someone wasn't ready to tell a story, I would not be the journalist coaxing, or persuading, or pushing them to confide in me. After all, I wasn't doing the kind of investigative journalism that shook up governments and exposed corruption. If they didn't want to go there, I didn't, because it was highly unlikely whatever it was they were hiding was in any genuine 'public interest'.

There were other times, though, when I would pursue a line of questioning if someone would allow me, which perhaps might feel a little uncomfortable. But this was for different reasons, because some stories are ready to share; we *want* to share them; but we aren't, because we're sabotaging.

Is it a wound or is it sabotage?

In storytelling, we talk about sharing the scar not the wound. This essentially means if you're still processing something you're going through, or are unhealed from a specific experience, it's perhaps not ready to share with the world yet. When we share something that we don't have a healthy perspective on, or are unable to see how we've learnt or grown or healed from that experience, you can risk losing your authority, and the people listening become voyeurs to your pain. In the past, I've followed the 'scar not a wound' rule pretty strictly. But I've since learnt this isn't always the case. Sometimes, you can share an experience or challenge in the moment or while you're still on the journey, not only because sharing it is cathartic for you, but because you sense sharing your experience may hold some value for others.

For most people, sharing their stories doesn't come naturally, particularly the more vulnerable parts of our journeys. So the majority of the time as a journalist, when I sensed there was something more to a story, I would keep asking questions, because I knew that often people wanted to share their stories, but didn't think they could. When I showed interest, asked the right questions and created a space in which someone could feel comfortable, however, so often a brilliant shining story they might never have told, would come spilling out.

When you're telling your own stories, you've got to create that space for yourself; you've got to ask yourself the right questions and decide whether you have the courage to give that story a platform. But before you can do that you have to work out *why* you are hiding in the first place.

That means that identifying the real reasons you're holding back is an important part of the puzzle to becoming a storyteller. Thankfully, the reasons we stay quiet are usually not that complicated or unique. In fact, the same things come up for different people time and again. Here are some of the most common themes I've encountered. You might find you identify with one of them, some of them, or even all of them to a certain extent, just like I do.

1. I'm Boring

I've lost count of the amount of times someone's told me they're embarrassed to share their story because it isn't interesting or exciting enough. Compared to half the world's population, personally I haven't had a particularly challenging or dramatic life either. I'm a middle class white woman living in Surrey in the UK – not really the makings of high drama. But not having had a dramatic past does not mean I haven't had challenges, learnt valuable lessons or had to heal. It doesn't mean I don't have stories that people want and need to hear. Everyone has a story that's valuable to someone else, and a message someone can only hear from you. That's because when you tell your story there will be someone out there who sees themselves in it, and perhaps for the first time, feels seen. For someone, your story will be a beacon of light.

LESSON
Your job isn't to judge your stories,
it's simply to tell them.

2. What will my friends and family think?

*'You own everything that happened to you.
Tell your stories.
If people wanted you to write warmly about them, they should have
behaved better.'*
- Anne Lamott, Author

I love this quote from Anne Lamott for its unapologetic commitment to story. It's true there are some situations where telling your story can affect other people, and sometimes we do need to think about whether we're willing to go there; the vast majority of the time though, that's not the case. The vast majority of the time, the real reason you're not telling stories is because you're *imagining* what your friends and family may think if you do, and often what you imagine is 100% wrong. Remember, those who really love you will respect what you share; the others won't be paying much attention to what you're doing at all; and the tiny percentage who *may* get annoyed, you weren't talking to them anyway.

Lesson
Don't let what other people
may or may not think
silence you.

There's a meme that goes around the Internet that's quite apt that goes something like this: *'If you're afraid your friends won't like you for speaking your truth, they never really liked you in the first place.'*

3. I'm scared I'll share something I'll regret

Ok. I'm not expecting you to reveal your most personal experiences on day one. As we've said, storytelling is a journey; in many ways it's an unravelling. It's ok, therefore, and probably preferable, to start off with small stories. I didn't launch straight in to telling people about my deepest wounds, and unless you really want to, you don't have to either. Start your storytelling journey with baby steps; tell a story about what happened at work today, not about the time your heart was broken in two. Knowing when a story is ready to tell is something we're going to talk more about in Chapter 6.

4. I don't want to look like I'm fishing for attention

You want to tell your story but you also don't want people thinking you're seeking sympathy, admiration or wanting to be made to feel special. This can be a big block to telling our stories, which is why it's really important to know the intention behind a story you share. Most of the time it's not because you want to share your drama (although sometimes it can be); most of the time, as we have already mentioned, sharing your story can be cathartic *and* help others.

5. I'm afraid that being vulnerable will undermine my authority.

Vulnerability is scary, but as we'll talk about more in the next chapter, it's also an important aspect of storytelling. Here's how I see vulnerability versus authority. In my work,

I'm constantly asking people to push their comfort zones; to go to places that perhaps are difficult to go. I ask them to get metaphorically naked with their message and their presence. When you're doing some kind of soul work, you're often challenging your audience in a similar way, so that's when it's helpful to remember that all communication is an energy exchange; a kind of karma, in that what you put out into the world, whether that's love, vulnerability and open-heartedness, or negativity, closed-mindedness and drama – that's what you get back. So, while you certainly don't want your therapist or coach to sit down in your session and tell you all about their troubles; for many people, knowing a person has once been where they now are, can be the reason they choose to sit down with them in the first place.

6. I censor what I talk about in case it offends someone

Let's hear it for the people-pleasers! In other words, those who deny themselves in order to make other people feel happy, safe or right. Speaking your truth can feel incredibly uncomfortable when you've spent a lifetime sitting on the fence and trying hard never to offend or annoy. Taking a stand for what you believe in, or quite simply unapologetically showing up as who you are, can be incredibly scary. But it's necessary, unless you want to live out your days for everyone but you. For me, talking about more metaphysical and spiritual things through my platform was a difficult decision. I was so fearful that the things I was interested in such as energy, vibration, astrology, quantum mechanics and metaphysics; which so inform the way I see the world, would offend or upset or attract judgement from dearly loved religious friends and family; or ridicule from others who just don't see the world in the same way. So, for years I kept that part of me hidden and out of my work, even though I felt strongly it was part of what I'm meant to do.

A great example of this is my friend the actress, presenter and Soulfire Sessions life and business coach, Lou George, who in 2021 began to use her platform to provide comment on the changing political landscape. Here's what she told me about this experience:

'I've always been a truth speaker, but previously it had always been in safe spaces with like-minded people. People try not to put their head above the parapet, but I believe we have to take self-responsibility and call out what we are seeing. I've always done this as a coach, but never commented on politics or the world situation before. But in this case so much was happening so quickly it brought a higher level of trust in myself, my voice and my power. I started Awakened Media to give a platform to the voices that weren't being heard, and because I was talking about things that were triggering and polarising for many, I received a lot of hurtful comments, and a tiny taste of what highly trolled people in the public eye must experience. At first it was upsetting, but I was so grounded in my truth that I eventually got a thicker skin, and I'm so grateful for that now, because I feel a much more confident and powerful woman as a result.'

7. I'm scared of being judged

Unfortunately, how people may react to our story is just something we can't control. People will judge. People will disagree with you. People may even be triggered and make nasty comments. The only thing you can truly control is how you tell your story, not how anyone receives it. So, stop worrying about things you can't control. Your job as a storyteller is to share your story with the right intentions; then all there is left to do is trust and surrender.

. . .

The Witch Wound

There are other things that can keep us silenced that may be out of your control. I first heard about the witch wound in Lisa Lister's book *Witch,* and it deeply resonated. If you're not familiar with the term, it refers to the phenomena where women find it hard to have a voice because of an ingrained generational fear around what has happened to outspoken women in the past.

There are some who will find this a far-fetched idea. Particularly today where this dark part of our history is often forgotten, minimised or romanticised. But the truth is, in the not-so distant past, thousands of women were killed or imprisoned for crimes such as 'witchcraft'; helping other women birth babies; for being outspoken, healing, or for simply not conforming to societal expectations. In some parts of the world, of course, this is still happening. Even in The West there are examples within my own lifetime, like the woman younger than my own grandmother, who spent her entire adult life in a mental asylum just a couple of miles up the road from where I grew up. She was not insane, rather her family placed her there for falling pregnant as an unmarried teen, and she never left.

Is it any surprise that fear to speak out and be different and shine, is still there inside many of us? Especially those who are doing the very work – healing, midwifery, astrology – they once would have been condemned for? But that fear can be true for any woman choosing to put their head above the parapet now. As Lisa says in *Witch,* that kind of fear is 'personal, societal, generational and matrilineal.'

Sharing your lived experience as a woman can still feel dangerous today. If that's how it feels to you right now, I hope this book will help you to start to feel courageous and sovereign and separate the real limits from the imagined. It should be safe to have a voice; it should be safe to share your story. And the best way for more men and women to feel this, is by leading by example. If you're still feeling censored or silenced, ask yourself why? Because although there are still cases of actual censorship at the time of writing this, often it's not outside forces that are keeping us silent, but our own fears and sabotages.

I hope you can now see why I've not just written a *how to write your story book*, and launched straight into a step-by-step of what to do. Because, yes you can learn how to tell a story, but having the *courage* to tell a story is completely different. Unfortunately, that's not something I can teach you, but hopefully some of the things I've talked about so far will help guide you on that journey. Before we move on, here are a few other things that have helped me to share my soul story, that may help you, too.

4 WAYS TO STOP HIDING & START SHINING

1. Get into alignment with who you really are

As someone who has committed a good chunk of the last few years to doing a lot of inner work, I know that the more I get to know myself, the better life becomes. But in knowing myself, it's also made clear the stories I want to tell. Writing and journalling is a powerful personal development tool to help you find that alignment.

Some questions that may be helpful to start with include:

- Where in my life am I not being true to myself?
- Where am I hiding?
- Why am I hiding and what am I scared of?

- Where am I not doing the work I really want to be doing?
- Who do I truly wish to speak to and inspire?
- Where does my message feel 'off?'
- Where have I adopted someone else's belief system, way of doing things, or way of being, rather than being true to my own?
- How can I be more fully myself when I show up?
- What am I here to do?

2. Remember that it's OK to share a story to heal yourself

Yes, share the scar not the wound or we risk turning our reader into a voyeur. But as we've already discussed, sharing a story that you're in the process of healing from can be cathartic and help others, too.

3. Allow your work to be all of you

When you create something, whether it's a business, a mission or a message, the easiest way to do that is by allowing it to be in flow. For me, that means my business is all of me. I curate what I share, but there's no part of me that doesn't fit into my business. It's your business; your soul work; your message; your life; your stories; so do what you want to do, and don't let anyone (including me) make you wrong.

4. Know your frequency

Understanding frequency and vibration has been a big journey for me the last decade, and I spend a lot of my time trying to make sure that in everything I do, from parenting to creating, that I'm operating from the highest vibration available to me. Drama is a low vibration; it's one of gossip and judgement and victimhood. Unfortunately, if you're creating content in the social media space it's easy to get caught up in drama. There are also lots of invitations for drama going on in our personal lives. When I tell stories and show up for my audience I want to be transparent, I want to be truthful, and I want to be sovereign. You can't be those things if you're also buying into drama. Know your highest frequency, and always show up for your life, and work from that place. We'll talk about this more in Chapter 8.

SUMMARY
STOP HIDING & START SHINING

If you're struggling to find your voice, ask yourself, *What's really keeping me hidden?* It's only really when you truly dig into what is really holding you back from sharing your stories, that you can decide if you have the courage to give your voice a platform.

So often, we are our own greatest censors.

———

CHAPTER 5
THE RULES OF STORY

W HAT MAKES A good story, and how do you decide if it's worth telling? Let's start with something that's at the heart of all good stories; you'll find it's also a thread that runs through all the other elements of good storytelling, too.

We've already talked a little bit about how some people are reluctant to share their stories due to a feeling of it not being enough. That's when you most need to remember this first important rule:

1. The best story is always the truest one.

I see storytelling more like truth-telling. Because no matter how ordinary your story may seem; no matter how tempting it is to make it a little more dramatic or elaborate, the best story is always the true one. And if you've chosen the right story for the right moment, that is the story that will land.

If we go back to the reason why humans have always been

drawn to story, it really comes down to a search for truth. And truth, like everything else in the world, has a vibration all of its own. The phrase 'that story doesn't ring true' is, in essence, what that means; in other words, *that story doesn't resonate because it lacks the vibration of truth.*

STORYTELLING IS REALLY TRUTH TELLING

What about fiction and fantasy? By definition, they are 'not true'. Obviously, this book deals with the stories of your lived experience, however, this rule applies to *all* stories. That's because it's not the magic, the drama or the adventure inside stories such as *The Lord of the Rings* or *Harry Potter* that make them great – those bits are just the frill and the fluff, no matter how fabulous. What really makes stories like these so power-ful, so timeless and so resonant, is the everyday truth that lies at the heart of them. The same goes for the stories of your life.

It's not the drama or glamour – it's the honesty, the inspiration, and the authenticity of your story that your audience will resonate with.

2. The best story brings value.

The content of the stories we tell have changed a lot over the generations, but one thing remains constant: story gives value to the reader. So whenever you tell a story, remember you are telling it *for* your reader, which means the first ques-tion you need to ask is:

What value does this story bring?

· · ·

Sometimes a story may be for pure entertainment purposes, something to amuse or amaze. But what we really want to be doing as leaders is going deeper than that. We want to:

- shift someone's perspective of a situation or challenge.
- illustrate a piece of wisdom or a concept someone's struggling to relate to or grasp.
- motivate, empower and inspire.

Whatever the reason you're sharing your story, it needs to be less about you, and more about your reader. Sharing your story should never be *'look at me; look at my pain, look at my success, my past and what I've survived,'* and should instead always be:

Learn from me; because this is what I know to be true.

3. A good story is vulnerable.

We've discussed how storytelling, in fact, how all communication, is an energy exchange. A bit like a recipe, the higher quality the ingredients, the more worthwhile the outcome. The same goes for vulnerability. The more vulnerable you are, the greater impact your story will have.

Vulnerability is not about handing over your power, though; it's about sharing from an empowered place, which we call empowered vulnerability. Brené Brown's *Daring Greatly* was pivotal in helping me see this for my own work. She says, *'Does showing up to be with someone in deep struggle sound like weakness? Is accepting responsibility weakness? No. Vulnerability sounds like truth and feels like courage. Truth and courage aren't always comfortable. But they are never weakness.'*

· · ·

4. A good story is personal.

The big mistake storytellers make is telling stories that other people have told before. While there's great value in fables and parables, so often we've heard them so many times that the meaning has lost its resonance; or those stories are so firmly rooted in a distant place or time that we can no longer relate to them. Even more recently, the starfish story or the story of the footprints in the sand (easily searchable online) are good examples. They're both good stories, but they don't have the same impact as they probably did the first time you heard them, or if the story was personal. And neither of these stories are personal; they may be told in the first person, but the 'I' in these stories isn't the storyteller themselves, and the story didn't really happen, it's a teaching aid or a parable. As a leader, what makes your story captivating, is when it shows what goes on behind the mask; the true you.

A good storyteller also understands that what's personal is universal. Details like being too shy to speak at networking events, or the mummy guilt that lands just after the kids go to bed, or eating a packet of biscuits because you're worried about money, or not going to the party because of what you see in the mirror. These things may feel extremely personal to you, like they're your darkest secrets, but in fact, these feelings aren't unique. Thousands, if not millions, of other people feel exactly the same way as you do, and when you reflect their lives, experience, deepest worries, thoughts, and peculiarities back at them through your story, that story becomes a connection, an affirmation, an outstretched hand that says, *you're not alone.*

LESSON

When you tell your story, you also tell someone else's.

The Invisible Chord

I pulled a few sickies when I was a child, and once feigned illness so I could stay off school and read the last few chapters of *Jane Eyre*. Incidentally, the reason I vividly remember this occasion is because my Mum (rightly suspicious), discovered my malingering after witnessing a rather dramatic recovery through the bedroom keyhole.

Anyway, if you're a Brontë fan you may also remember the line where Rochester talks of the string or 'cord of communion' linking him and Jane. At 10 years old I knew he was talking metaphorically, but while I won't go so far as to suggest Charlotte Brontë knew anything about quantum entanglement, I now suspect Mr Rochester was also talking energetically.

Lovers, friends, enemies aren't the only people we create energetic cords with though. When we tell a story that resonates with someone, that makes them feel seen, we also create an energetic cord between us and them. This is particularly important to remember when we're sharing stories as a leader or business owner.

Of course, it's easier to just share the bare facts with your audience. For example:

> In 2018, I left my career in journalism to start a business teaching copywriting to online business owners.

It's true. But that's not going to create much of a connection, no 'cord of communion' is going on there. When I tell the same story differently, however, about how I started a business when my son was six months old because I didn't want to go back to work and leave him; how I knew that I was meant to do something different with my life; how I thought, well if there's never a good time to start a business, why not then? That resonated with a lot of people. My audience, mainly women, all entrepreneurs, often mothers, could see themselves in that story, which created a connection; an invisible cord. Because when you tell your story, you also tell someone else's. They feel seen by you; and *they're more likely to like* you, because *you're like them.*

SUMMARY

- The best story is always the truest one (not the most dramatic or glamorous)
- Stories should bring value – sometimes it will be purely for entertainment, but most of the time there will be a lesson of some sort.
- Being vulnerable is powerful and empowering.
- Share details – particularly the ones that will mirror your audience's own experiences.

———

PART TWO
YOUR STORY GOLDMINE

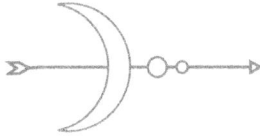

CHAPTER 6
THE STORIES YOU'RE READY TO TELL

NOW IT'S TIME to crack things open and get all your most powerful and inspiring stories spilling out of you like one big soul-shaped piñata. This is where we're also going to talk about how to start cultivating a creator's mindset, and about when and why you should (or shouldn't) tell a particular story. But first, let's start off very simply with the stories you can start telling right now.

Whether you're a business owner, a healer, a therapist, a coach, a maker, a creator, an activist, or a campaigner, the most obvious story you'll want to tell, or perhaps already are, is the journey that led you to where you are right now. Maybe you've shared this story already and it hasn't had much of an impact. That doesn't mean it won't ever. As you'll learn, there are several ways to tell the story of your journey to now; but first, let's look at three of the most common reasons your story may not have had the impact you desired in the past.

3 REASONS YOUR STORY DIDN'T WORK

1. *You think that what matters most to you, also matters most to your audience.*

Getting the hook of your story right is so important. The hook of a story is the thing that grabs people's attention and draws them in, much like a fishing rod. Sometimes, working out the hook is easy, because the aspect of your story which is most important to you, also happens to be the part of your story that will resonate most with your audience. When that's the case, happy days!

But sometimes it isn't that simple. And if we don't work out the one thing in our story that is going to truly resonate with our audience, and lead with that, it doesn't matter how fantastically told, your story will fall on deaf ears (We'll talk about how to work out the right story for the right audience in Chapter 9, Story-Storming).

2. You've confused your story with the chronology of your life

The stuff on your CV isn't your story, and if you boil yourself down to a few qualifications and a bunch of job titles, you're almost certainly selling yourself short. You are a multi-dimensional being and your past is vast. By the time you hit 40, all the things that have led to here are already a thousand strands of stories, woven into one. Even if you think hardly anything's happened, you will still have a very full back story with twists and turns and highs and lows; people entering stage left and exiting stage right; paths veering off and new ones opening up; and there will have been multiple beginnings and endings. Your back story isn't one story, it's many stories all ravelled into one thick rope. And if you don't know how, that can be quite an overwhelming thing to boil down into something short and engaging. That's one of the reasons so many people resort to relaying their story in terms of the chronological milestones of their career path (the other reason being a tendency to hide behind expertise). But telling your story like this is the quickest way for an audience to forget you.

LESSON

Good storytelling is about picking the right story for the right situation.

3. You're not sharing it enough

Telling your story isn't one and done. Just because you shared it in an email once, or even in a book or on social media a few times, doesn't mean you shouldn't tell it again. In fact, all great leaders tell their stories over and over, often until their audience is able to repeat that story for them. When you tell your story enough, it becomes your signature story; you become the coach, healer, teacher, leader, entrepreneur, artist who… (fill in the blank). In other words, that story has the power for you to be seen in a certain light. It can also anchor you in your audience's psyche as someone who represents a certain set of values or principles; often someone who is a beacon of hope because you have done the things they dream of doing, in spite of challenges, circumstances or backgrounds, that may or may not be similar to their own.

Take Gabby Bernstein, the one-time alcohol-addicted party-girl turned spiritual guru. Elizabeth Gilbert, who famously travelled the world to escape an unhappy marriage and found herself (as recounted in her bestselling memoir, *Eat, Pray, Love*).

Oprah Winfrey is another good example. Her story of pregnant teen born into rural poverty to self-made billionaire philanthropist, is not only a journalist's and biographer's dream, but is a story that allows one of the world's wealthiest celebrities to still be considered by her audience as 'one of us'.

———

YOUR FIRST 3 STORIES

So, we've established that you have a very full back story, made up of thousands of story threads. We're going to be talking about how to work out which story strand to pull and how to tell that story in a way they'll remember it later. But for now, let's start off with three simple stories you already have, and how to work out which strands of your past make them up.

The examples I'm going to give may seem specifically geared to business owners, but the truth is they can be applied to anyone doing anything. You could be part of a charity, run a foundation, be a member of an organisation, a group, a club; or be an enthusiast of some sort, it doesn't matter, you'll have these three stories ready to tell and regularly draw on.

Firstly, I'm going to run through what each story is, and then I'm going to run through a series of questions that will help you figure out what are the bones of each story. We're not talking about how to write or tell your story yet, we're simply working out which elements go into each one.

1. **The Founder's Story**

This one's a given. Every business had a moment where it didn't exist in the founder's mind, and a moment when it suddenly did. Every idea wasn't there one moment, and was taking shape the next. Every new activity or interest in your life was born out of somewhere. The moment it came into being is the essence of your founding story.

To keep things simple we'll focus on a business; the founding story of your business is essentially how your business was born. It's the story of the moment where you realise that you might be onto something.

The founding story of Amazon, for example, happens when Wall Street employee Jeff Bezos is on a cross-country road trip and hits on the idea to start an online bookshop from his garage.

The founding story of entrepreneur Jenna Kutcher takes place when she was a successful but steadily burning out wedding photographer, who decides to start teaching how she has grown and marketed a successful business instead.

Outlining your Founder's Story

1. Describe the moment you realised there was a business or if you're not a business owner, some kind of potential, in what you do now?

Maybe it was a conversation you had, a lightbulb moment when reading a book or watching a movie; maybe it was the gazillionth time someone wanted to pick your brains about a particular subject.

Or perhaps it's when you finally came out the other side of a problem you'd worked hard to solve.

Tip: Try to identify the specific moment the idea for your

business or venture came to you. What triggered the idea? What did that moment look like?

> 2. Which event or series of events directly led you to that moment?

So, for example, if you help women heal a specific condition by teaching them how to nourish their bodies with natural foods, perhaps the events that led up to this was how you had experienced the same symptoms and had then sought your own solutions.

> 3. What does that business or idea look like right now?

In other words, what is the manifestation of this idea now? What do you do? Who do you help and how?

Once you've written down those 3 things, you have the bones of your *Founder's Story.* Keep it safe. You'll come back to it later.

2. **The Purpose Story**

This is your North Star story. It's the reason why you do what you do, which, by the way is not just about delivering x to y. Your purpose story is the greater reason behind your business; the thing that drives you to get up at 5am, or work until midnight; it's the inspiration; it's what makes your work so aligned. For most people who are doing work they love, AKA their soul work, the purpose of their work isn't just money, because you can make money doing a thousand different things. There's a reason why you choose to make money *this* way.

> *For example, my purpose, and the reason I wrote this book, is because I want to help more visionaries and*

heart-led leaders become voices for positive change by teaching them how to tell their stories.

Your purpose is the reason behind why you do what you do, and as you grow your business or mission, your purpose is not only going to inspire your message, but it's going to inspire everyone whose lives your work touches, too.

The 5 Whys Exercise

It's not always easy to clarify your one specific purpose. We often stand for so many things, that trying to distil everything that we are into one single purpose can be tricky. A great way to help you quickly get to the heart of your purpose (or your current purpose as this often changes as we grow) is the 5 Whys exercise.

You may already be familiar with this – it's an exercise commonly used in corporate training environments to help employees get to the crux of a problem or idea. It's a very simple exercise:

Step 1:

You take a problem – in our case – what is your purpose? And you ask the question *Why? Why do I do what I do?*

Step 2:

You answer your question and then whatever that answer is, you again ask why, framing the question in response to your answer.

Step 3:

Ask the question why 3 more times, each time framing the question in response to your most recent answer.

·   ·   ·

For example:

WHY DID I START MY BUSINESS?

Answer 1:

Because I wanted to teach visionaries, creatives and change-makers how to become better communicators

WHY?

Answer 2:

So that they can reach more people with their message

WHY?

Answer 3:

Because so many of them are doing amazing things, but just aren't able to explain what they offer in a way that gets people's attention.

WHY?

Answers 4:

Because everybody has a platform these days, but not everyone has found their voice, and I want to help them to do that.

WHY?

Answer 5:

Because the more independent and diverse voices there are making an impact in the world, the faster we can build a better one.

Once you've completed the above exercise, answer the following questions:

1. What is the purpose behind your business?
2. What was the incident/ realisation/ or series of events that made you realise this was your purpose?
3. How does that purpose play out in your business now?

You now have the elements that make up your purpose story. Again, hang on to this, because you'll be able to come back and put it all together as a story, later.

Finally, let's talk about an all-important story that is a little bit harder to pin down, but once you do, is absolute gold.

1. **The Sticky Story**

Your sticky story is the thing that people remember you for. It's when they say, *'I know Laura, she's the life coach or healer who…'* That's your sticky story. And that's the story you can use on your website About page, a sales page, a bio, when you appear on a podcast, or as part of a TEDX. Your sticky story blends the heart of who you are with what you do.

So, let's look at how you can use elements of both your founder and purpose stories to create your Sticky Story.

• • •

Outlining your Sticky Story

It's not uncommon for your sticky story to be all about becoming a beacon of hope. As leaders, we've often been through a transformation ourselves that reflects our own customer's journey in some way. Very often this is a critical moment in our life; a health crisis; a relationship break down; a moment where everything has fallen apart. But, as we will discuss, the inciting incident doesn't have to be big and dramatic to be life-changing – it could simply be a matter of choosing to do something differently or following a gut feeling (remember the best story is always the true one). Either way, this transformation we have gone through is an A to B journey that may also reflect the journey our audience hopes to go on by following your work. By sharing your journey, therefore, you are:

- **Giving them hope…** They think, 'She's done it, maybe I can, too?'
- **Showing that you understand them…** They think, 'She's been here; she gets me.'
- **Building your authority….** They think, 'She knows how to get out the other side of this challenge and can show me how.'

As we've discussed, while you most likely want to make money from your business or project (whether as a personal salary or to fund a cause), money isn't the only reason it exists. In fact, your current mission was probably born in one of two ways:

1. **From your own personal transformation.**

Starting a business or project after a personal transformation is really common, particularly in the coaching, healing and service-based industries. It usually goes something like this: In the past you've faced a particular challenge or problem; you've worked to overcome it; and now you share the tools you used or created to solve that problem or challenge to help other people transform their lives in the same way.

> If this is you, your sticky story is your own
> A to B transformation.

Sharing the story of your own transformation is so powerful, because it helps your customers and clients not only realise you understand them, but it helps them see themselves in your journey, and envision exactly what's possible.

Or, you're an expert and you have...

2. A Calling

Experts with a calling usually have a specific skill set and knowledge base that they've used for years, and for some reason have decided to start a business so they could use those skills to solve a specific problem for a specific type of person.

> If this is you, your Sticky Story is the moment you realised your
> true purpose, and the seed of your business was born

This is also a powerful story, because you're not only establishing yourself as an expert, but an expert who was driven to do what they do out of a sense of passion and purpose.

Finding the Golden Thread

Back at the start of this chapter, we talked about how one of the reasons a story may not resonate with an audience is not understanding which thread of your story matters to them most. This can be a common stumbling block when trying to work out your sticky story, particularly if you belong to the *'expert with a calling'* group. That's because often your journey won't reflect that of your clients or audience in an obvious way. That doesn't mean, however, that there isn't something that's going to resonate. In fact, there almost certainly is! Your job is to identify the element or thread of your story that reflects their journey, desires, challenges or beliefs in some way – let's call this *'the golden thread.'*

Finding my golden thread actually happened by accident. I didn't even know I was looking for it or needed one. You've heard how back in the early days of my business I was doing a whole lot of hiding. This meant that storytelling was not yet a big part of my communications; teaching copywriting, I did a whole lot of hiding behind copywriting skills and informative content marketing. I shared my founder's story of course, but as a classic 'expert with a calling', while my founding story of being a journalist who applied her knowledge of writing and content creation to teaching entrepreneurs content marketing, was an authority builder, it didn't create that heart-to-heart connection that's so important.

Then one day, I sat down to rewrite my 'About' page on my website, and suddenly it all just clicked. I'd been running my business for a year or so by then, worked with handful of private clients and done tons of group work. As a stream of consciousness, I wrote about my own journey to here, and realised that, while I've been writing and communicating my whole working life, there was one thing I had in common with my audience; I had discovered that being an effective communicator, wasn't just about being a good writer, speaker or having the correct marketing formula. Being a good communicator was all about having the insight, self-awareness and courage to unapologetically share your voice, your story and put yourself out there.

That, was what I had in common with my audience: I understood that showing up and sharing your story and putting yourself out there takes guts and courage, and finding that courage can be hard. This was something I'd experienced myself; had watched interviewees grapple with back in my journalism days; and was something I'd instinctively always guided my clients and students through. I hadn't actually realised how important it was though, and that realisation not only shaped the story I started sharing about myself, but gave me clarity on what really made me different in my niche.

Ok, let's start putting your sticky story together now by answering the following questions:

1. Which part of your journey most closely reflects the A to B transformation your clients or audience will go on with you?
2. Which event, crisis or incident in your past has fundamentally moulded who you are right now?

Remember, this doesn't have to be a big dramatic event to have been critical moment or incident. For me, it was starting my business and knowing all the skills I needed to market myself, but realising that the tools without the courage, confidence and clarity, weren't enough.

3. What did your life look and feel like before this event?

4. What does your life look like now?

5. What were the challenges you had to overcome on this journey?

6. How has this affected your worldview?

7. What does this make you expert in, or how does this make you different to other experts in your field?

Now you have the bones of your Founder's Story, your Purpose Story and your Sticky Story. Keep them safe, because when we move on to Part 3 – 'Story Craft' – you'll learn exactly how to take those outlines, and turn them into compelling stories.

SUMMARY

THE STORIES YOUR READY TO TELL

You have hundreds of stories to tell, but you already have three really obvious ready-made stories, you can start telling right now.

These are:

Your founder's story (how you started your business)

Your purpose story (the why behind your business)

Your sticky story a little harder to pinpoint, but this is a combination of the first two stories, plus that thing that makes you different and gets you remembered.

———

CHAPTER 7
MAGIC, MEMORY & EVERYDAY MOMENTS

WHEN I WAS TINY, perhaps barely three years old, my next-door neighbour was everything a granny ought to be; she had white candyfloss hair and a soft round tummy; she wore brooches on her cardigans and kept a packet of digestive biscuits in a cake tin painted with yellow roses. Her name was Mrs Baughan, but when I learnt to talk she became just 'Baughan' to me. My siblings and I adored her, as did our mother for whom she was always on hand with a kind word, some good advice, or an offer to watch the baby – who was me.

I perhaps hadn't thought of Baughan for a good few years before I first started teaching story. She'd died after moving to the West Country to live with her daughter when I was still very small. But one day when I was thinking about the intricate tapestry that is our past – the thousand strands of story that make up each life – I suddenly had a strong memory of being in the garden of Baughan's bungalow. In my memory, I am wearing a little blue cotton pinafore dress and I am crawling along the garden path, exploring every inch of it on my hands and knees. This is not because I hadn't learnt to walk yet, but because unlike the unremarkable greyish square slabs in my own grandmother's garden, or the ubiquitous crazy paving next door in ours, Baughan's path was made up of magic and memory. Set into the concrete between the worn red bricks and shiny cobble stones, were countless little treasures that Baughan had salvaged, saved or even dug up from her garden: the round dimpled bases of glass bottles and jars; smashed fragments of willow-patterned china; a couple of chipped ceramic tiles with faded pictures of little Dutch girls and clover. And all the way along the edge were hundreds of brown, rust and caramel-coloured pebbles, laid out in waves and sunbursts.

I'm not sure how many garden paths I can remember after five minutes, but Baughan's I can still remember after 38 years. Is memory perfect? No. Have the years embellished its magic? Perhaps, I honestly don't know. But the point is, I remember it like this. Not because it was the most stylish or expertly crafted, not because it led anywhere particularly unusual (the washing line, in fact), but because it was totally unique; a path I'd never seen the like of before, and have never seen since. That is the same difference between a story that gets remembered, and a story that gets forgotten or ignored – it's one you've never heard before, and perhaps never have since. And that is why great communicators don't repeat stories someone else has already told;

> Great communicators share their message and their ideas in the context of who they are, by telling their own stories.

Your audience doesn't need ground-breaking new tips or never-heard-before wisdom; they just need to hear the same few important lessons and ideas repeated in fresh new ways, and there's nothing more fresh or original than your lived experience. No-one has the collection of moments that you've lived; no-one has experienced life from your point of view.

That's why digging deeper into what you know and all the little things you've done becomes such a valuable source of content for a communicator. It doesn't matter what your field is or your niche, the stories you tell don't have to fit that theme – in fact, it's better if they don't, especially if your audience isn't expert in your field. This means you can be talking about corporate leadership, and find the perfect anecdote from the playground 40 years before; or share a lesson in health or spirituality, framed by a story about what happened in the supermarket this morning, or a conversation you overheard in the gym. When we take moments like this and use them as a hook for a story, we call it *everyday moment storytelling*. This is where we take inspiration from something that has happened to us recently, which has either taught us a lesson, shifted our perception, or is quite simply the perfect hook or illustration of a message we wish to share.

Everyday Moment Storytelling

The character Carrie Bradshaw in the TV show *Sex and the City* was a newspaper columnist and a prolific everyday moment storyteller. In nearly every episode she seemed to be sitting at her typewriter relaying some life event, and then linking it to a lesson or message with phrases like *'which got me thinking about…'* or *'which made me realise that…'*. Carrie used her everyday life as constant inspiration. Similarly, my everyday life is one of the most abundant sources of inspiration for communicating with my audience. If you subscribe to my newsletter, you'll find my emails will often start with sentences such as *'I was reading a book to my daughter tonight….'*, or *'My husband said to me today…'*. It's an approach that comes naturally and easily to me because I see my life as a collection of lessons and stories – your life is too, you've just got to start looking for them. There is of course another advantage that everyday moment storytelling brings to your communications, and that is that it's not only an elegant and engaging way to frame value, but it's also an opportunity to give your audience a little peak behind the curtain of your life. Take them with you to the bookshop; on your walk in the woods; tell them what happened at the supermarket; about the conversation you had with your friend at yoga class. Often these stories are less significant in themselves, and more like hooks or jumping off points that allow you to share an insight, opinion, lesson or view that will enrich the life or day of your reader in some way.

Look for the universal

As a writer I've always looked for the magic in the mundane and, in reverse, the ordinary in the extraordinary. Partly because I'm a total day dreamer, but also because when it comes to story, it creates a potent balance. While we all love to read about filmstars and icons and their extraordinary lives, the parts of their lives that resonate and connect are the places where they overlap with our own lives – where they are exquisitely ordinary. We realise that *perhaps they're not so different from us after all.* Equally stories of ordinary people doing incredible things gives us a sense that, *yes, maybe we too have the potential to be extraordinary.*

The thing that these two scenarios have in common is the universal. There are certain experiences that almost everybody can relate to regardless of sex, cultural background or social standing. For example, being the new student in class; falling in love; not getting the job; having your heart broken. When we frame our message and teachings in universal scenarios, we create a powerful tool for connection, that can also be used to help make even the most alien, unusual, complex or intangible concepts something your audience can finally grasp. Looking for the universal is about drawing on everything around you, whether it's rights of passage, types of people we all have in our lives, or even something very mundane and common place, like being a small child playing on the garden path.

Which stories should you tell?

So, which of those thousands of stories that have made up your life so far are the ones you should start to tell? As a general rule you want to be telling stories that…

- Help people to understand who you are, where you come from and what has shaped your worldview.
- Show what your values are and how you live them out.
- Can be used to illustrate abstract concepts and turn them into tangible experiences and ideas.
- Give commonly recognised ideas and old wisdom a new take.
- Show what you stand for.
- Give your audience an insight into your own growth and journey – truly inspiring leaders are transparent, open, constantly growing and learning.

Tell stories about what you know.

The best storytellers tell stories about what they know – so what do you know? Not just as a professional or an expert, but as a person. Maybe it's grief, maybe it's hope, maybe it's transformation, love, anger, fear, addiction, abuse, healing, jealousy, pain. Maybe it's all these things, since these are universal experiences that we all have to a greater or lesser degree. The real question is, which of these experiences matter to you and to your audience most? And which stories can you tell to bring them to life?

That's what story-storming will help you with, and it's what we'll be talking about in Chapter 8, but first let's talk about something that to me is so important as a storyteller: The hidden power inside every story you tell.

SUMMARY

MAGIC, MEMORY & EVERYDAY STORYTELLING

- The best communicators share stories that only they can tell – stories drawn from their unique histories, backgrounds and worldview – this is what gets a story remembered.
- Your audience doesn't have to be the same as you to connect with you; what's personal is universal, so when you share your feelings, emotions and experiences in an authentic way, that's what makes a story resonate.

———

CHAPTER 8
THE HIDDEN ENERGY OF STORY

THIS IS THE MOMENT I hear my brother saying, in a grave movie-trailer voice, *'With great power comes great responsibility....'* Rather embarrassingly, it was a fairly recent discovery of mine that this wisdom did not originate from *The Spiderman* franchise. But anyway, whoever said it first – Franklin D. Roosevelt, Peter Parker's Uncle Ben or some dude in a toga – they were all right. As storytellers (the most powerful people in the world, remember?), we must be conscious and intentional about how we show up, because all communication is energy and, as I learnt in a rather dramatic fashion the year before I began my business, stories in particular can entirely change the shape of someone's world.

In 2017, two things happened in my life: I had my second baby, a little boy (which meant I now had two small children I couldn't stop kissing); and as my heart swelled to an impossible size, my anxiety mushroomed out of control. Anxiety wasn't new to me, it had always been lingering at a low-level somewhere beneath the surface. I don't know if it was post-pregnancy hormones, tiredness or both, but suddenly the world seemed more dangerous than ever, and fear and anxiety hijacked every piece of happiness I had. Having worked in the media, I'd always habitually watched, listened to or read the news throughout the day – but had it always been filled with so much death, tragedy, cruelty and disaster?

When I took my children to the park or the shops, I'd have horrific premonitions of what might happen should I cross the road at the wrong moment, or if I lost sight of them in the playground. When my husband worked away from home I'd spend hours of the night awake, convinced something terrible had happened to him. I worried about our health – what if I got ill? What if he got ill? What would happen to the kids? On the outside I put on a brave face, but on the inside I felt fractured, terrified and totally out of control. I finally confided in a health visitor at the baby clinic, who had casually asked if everything was ok. I responded with a tight little shake of my head and a betrayingly high voice.

No, things really were not ok.

We then went on to establish that, *yes my husband was loving and supportive; yes, everyone was healthy and well; and yes, I was surrounded by plenty of amazing family and friends.* Basically, anxiety aside, my life was a peach. She suggested I book to see my GP. But as I walked home from that appointment, my son strapped to my chest and my little girl picking the daisies and dandelions from the grass verge as we went, I realised something that totally changed how I saw the world around me.

My life *was* happy. On paper, I was probably the most content I'd ever been, and yet it all felt precarious and fragile. Why was that? Not because it was. No. But because I was surrounded by a disproportionate number of negative narratives and stories, and the constant bombardment had slowly distorted my experience until I didn't feel or believe the truth in front of my own eyes. The power of story had shape-shifted my reality. And in identifying the problem, I also found the cure.

Stories have the power to change our entire experience,
so we must be conscious of the stories we consume and the
stories we share

When I thought about it, there had been a lot going on in the world – by 2017 standards anyway. There was the war in Syria, Brexit and all the vitriol from both sides, a spate of global terrorist events including the bombing of the Ariana Grande concert, and a few miles from where I lived, many had been killed in a fire in a block of high-rise flats. I'd followed it all every single day, immersed myself in the stories and cried for the lives lost and ruined. Was it any wonder I was feeling brittle? As humans, we were not designed to carry the burdens of the entire world, and yet an entire world of stories can be delivered to your phone in seconds.

I decided to edit the narratives and stories that were shaping my life; anything that fed my fears, anxiety or made me feel unsafe, I would remove or minimise until I felt better. Obviously the first thing that had to go was the news. I turned off the television, switched off notifications, and swapped the radio for a Spotify playlist (if the world was about to end, surely someone would let me know); I carefully curated my social media channels, and when friends or family stepped into drama, or started talking about terrible and depressing things, I'd steer the topic away. Slowly my internal balance restored; the sky looked blue again, and I could finally enjoy all my blessings without feeling terrified that I was about to lose them. This was a powerful shift, and the first nudge towards understanding how the energy and intention we hold when we communicate, matters as much as the words.

Sticks and Stones

When Dr Masaru Emoto carried out a series of experiments exploring how external influences affect water, he exposed the water to positive and negative words and feelings, then shock froze the water so he could study the impact on its molecular structure. What he found was that the water molecules exposed to positive words and feelings such as love, peace and gratitude, formed the most beautiful symmetrical shapes; while the water exposed to negative ideas, such as hate and judgement, froze into ugly, chaotic patterns. With a quick search online you can look it up and see for yourself.

When I discovered this, the first thing I thought about was how wise our ancestors had been to bless their food, and how perhaps there was something in holy water after all. But then remembering that the human body is made up of roughly 60% water itself, I realised that the energy and feelings we expose ourselves to have a huge impact. '*Sticks and stones may break my bones, but words will never hurt me,*' couldn't be further from the truth. Words and stories can have a positive or a negative impact, and as storytellers we must be conscious about the energy with which we share them.

You are the red sock

Everyone knows what it's like to feel a subtle or not-so

subtle shift in how you feel after a particular interaction. Some interactions leave no trace at all, while others energise you, and others still can drain or depress, make you feel fearful or even angry. That's because every time we write an email, share a blog post or social media update, or even just have a conversation on the phone, we're projecting out into the world whichever energy we hold in our body, and the reality is most people don't take responsibility for the energy they're putting out into the world.

Ironically, this includes large parts of our media (the traditional and the new) as well the advertising industry, which makes money from fear, scarcity and lack. It doesn't take a genius to work out that these business's follow a revenue over responsibility model; they know that ideas and stories that induce fear, anxiety, polarisation and division, sell more papers, get more clicks, shift more products. What does it matter if it makes a few people a little more scared, a little more anxious, a little more inadequate; it's good for business. Of course, as purpose-driven entrepreneurs, teachers and visionaries, we're not in the communications game for the likes and the clicks, we're in it to share a message and make positive change in the world. As conscious leaders, we all have to remember that we're the red sock in the white wash, which means we have the power to colour and change the tone of somebody's entire being through the stories and messages we choose to share with them, and the energy we share them with.

The Story Contract

The internet is the great connector, and with it, as a leader, you have the potential to create your own mini media empire. You don't have to be a news outlet or a movie star to reach thousands or even millions of people every day – in fact, there are several influencers whose reach rivals that of many traditional media outlets. But whether your ambitions are to be the next Oprah, the next Gabby Bernstein, or you just want to grow a small but loyal band of followers who need your message and support, you can help to set a new precedent – one where we at least take responsibility for how we show up and the energy we share with the world. For me, this means that before showing up I tune in to myself and ask, *Am I coming from a place of fear; scarcity; anger; closed mindedness or judgement?* Because that is *not* the energy I want to pass on. Sometimes the answer will be *No, I'm not,* but because I'm only human with highs and lows (and hormones), sometimes the answer is *Yes, I am.* And if I catch that, that's when I delete the email, close the message, stop talking, leave the story for another day. It's not fool proof, we make mistakes. But every day I show up and do what I can to honour that contract.

This doesn't mean you have to stick to uncontroversial topics. I am not advocating spiritual bypassing or being an ostrich. We absolutely *can* and *must* educate ourselves and talk about the serious stuff – after all part of a true light worker's mission is to shine light on the shadow. The difference is this; just as we choose not to consume those stories from a place of fear, we shouldn't share stories in a way that unnecessarily fuels somebody else's fear. You can't guarantee this will never happen again, but you *can* choose to be intentional and always, always show up from a place of love.

How to tune into your heart voice

Coming from a place of love doesn't mean being soft or weak. Yes, love is patient, love is kind, but love is also passionate, resonant, strong, truthful, courageous and fierce. When you come from a place of love you are speaking with your heart voice, and it has a completely different vibration; one of truth, integrity and compassion. Your heart voice never speaks from a place of fear or judgement. Right now, we are moving out of the age of the ego and into the age of the heart, and so tuning into that heart voice is something every leader needs to start to do. Here's a great journalling exercise to help you hear and see and feel the difference between the voice that comes from our head, and the voice that comes from our heart space.

THE HEART VOICE EXERCISE

1. Pose yourself a journalling question.

2. Take two chairs. The first will represent your head voice, the second your heart voice. In the first chair, journal the answer to your question, using your head voice. This is usually the automatic voice we use for our own internal chatter. Once you're done, move into the second chair.

3. When you finish, move to the second chair, but before you start writing, this time stabilise your breathing; place your hand on your heart and tune into your heart's intelligence.

4. Journal the answer to the same question, but this time know you are using your heart voice.

5. Once both pieces of journaling are complete, compare the two.

Most people will find there is a definite difference; the difference between sharing from your head, and your heart.

CHAPTER 9

STORY-STORMING – HOW TO MINE FOR STORIES & TURN THEM INTO VALUABLE CONTENT

S TORY-STORMING IS how you unearth and take an inventory of your story goldmine. What makes the process so exciting and rewarding, is that you not only realise just how many potential anecdotes and stories are already available to you and ready to weave into your content, but it's also an opportunity to start building a bank of stories for you to draw from in the future.

How to approach the Story-Storming exercise

Before you start, I want to make it clear that we are not looking for fully formed stories at this point. Simple notes like, *'The time I tried belly dancing'*, *'When my youngest child swallowed his first tooth'*, or *'The woman I met walking the dog last year,'* is enough. Don't worry that you have no idea how it could ever relate to anything you'd want to share with your audience – if that memory rises to the surface, just note it down. My belief is that these memories have come up because there's a lesson or a meaning hidden in them some-where for you and quite possibly a lesson that can be shared.

What that lesson is may be obvious, but if it isn't, don't worry. Just bring the memory forward in your internal filing system by recording it in a document or notebook, and you'll be surprised which stories from your past suddenly are the perfect match for a particular piece of content. You also don't have to go into great detail while recording your story (unless you think you might forget important things). The goal of Story-Storming is not to write up your stories, but to get as many story ideas down in one session as possible.

The easiest approach is to start by methodically working through all the different areas in your life – the people, the places, the possessions, the experiences etc, and taking note of any memories and moments that you associate with them. Choose a dedicated notebook, create a Word file, or a spreadsheet – it doesn't matter how you record them, just get them down.

How long should you spend StoryStorming?
I'd suggest setting aside an initial hour to do this exercise, and then once that's done you can add to your list of stories as more ideas emerge.

Getting Started
Below are 9 suggested areas to help give your session structure and get the ideas flowing, but if you'd like a more comprehensive list of questions to guide you through, you can download my Story-Storming Playbook for free with your other book bonuses at www.theluminous.media/bonus.

STORYSTORMING

1. *Your Highs and Lows*

Life has peaks and troughs; and those highs and lows are rich with story potential, because so often these moments are where we learn our most obvious lessons. Think about mistakes you've made, achievements you're proud of, the worst things that have happened to you and the best things that have happened to you. Which stories, moments and memories come up?

2. *Your Working Life*

The time we spend working takes up a huge proportion of our lives, and as a result it's rich with stories – dramatic ones, funny ones, sad ones, poignant ones. From first jobs and worst jobs, to colleagues and bosses, the good and the bad. Like me you've probably done a lot of jobs – I've been a barmaid, a silver service waitress, stuffed envelopes for a stationery company, sold natural skincare products, and handed out flyers outside The Royal Albert Hall, among other things.

My first ever job though, was a paper round. In fact, I had two paper rounds, both on a Thursday night, and at 14 years old I was the only one of my friends with a job, which they all thought was hilarious. Not because I had a job, but because I didn't actually do my paper round on my own. In fact, my mum, Nan *and* Grandad used to help me. Every Thursday after school, we'd load up my Grandad's black cab with stacks of newspapers and leaflets, and drive around street to street, each taking a different side of the road, to get the job finished in record time, so we could all go home for a cup of tea and dinner. I dreaded those Thursdays back then. But funnily enough I look back on them now with such huge nostalgia and fondness. I love the memory of that family team effort. I love the fact that for my Nan and Grandad, I know it was something they actually looked forward to. I was so lucky. I'm not sure what I'll use that little story for yet, but it's there in my bank waiting for the right moment... maybe this is it.

3. People in your life

List out all the most important people in your life now and from your past, and think about all of the stories you can think of related to them. I use stories from people in my life often – my childhood next-door neighbour and grandparents have come up already in the last few chapters. In fact, a few years back I was commissioned to write a piece called 'Playing Truant' for *The Simple Things* magazine, all about the importance of stepping away from normal life and just having fun. In that article, I wrote about my Grandad who was a London cabbie, and the morning he was driving across Waterloo Bridge ready to start a day's work, when he suddenly performed a U-turn in the road (or so I like to imagine) so he could head home to take us all down to the seaside for the day instead.

The moment my Grandad, Eddie, walked back in through the front door, dumped his big black leather coin sack on the counter and said to general astonishment, *'Let's go to Brighton!'* went down in Butler family legend. One moment we were squabbling over a board game, and the next we were piling into his cab ready for a day on the beach, playing in the arcades, riding the fairground, and eating fish and chips out of polystyrene trays on the pier.

The memories brought up by the people in our lives can often be the most potent. Don't forget to think about the minor characters or less obvious people from your past as well, such as old neighbours, parents of childhood friends, and even ancestors you never met.

. . .

4. Places

Places such as homes and houses we've lived in and the schools we went to, can hold a strong nostalgia and a huge amount of memories that you thought you'd forgotten. If you're struggling, do a little virtual tour of the rooms in your mind's eye – think about the different areas of your school – the corridors; the classrooms; the playground; think about your childhood bedroom. Also think about places you may only have been once or twice – holiday destinations, day trips – places that inspired you, scared you, or where you felt most at home.

5. Emotions and Health

Another great way to access stories from your past that you've perhaps forgotten is to think about feelings. Times you were sad, angry, disappointed, embarrassed. Or think about your health – when have you struggled with your health and are there are any stories there?

6. Possessions

What things do you have about you: items you've inherited; objects you've had for years; things that are valuable to you either in sentiment or price; items you use every day; gifts you've given and received; stuff you've collected, lost and found.

7. Life events

Anniversaries, deaths, births, big birthdays, retirements – what happened? Because the story probably isn't the occasion itself, but something unexpected or poignant that happened there that gave you a lesson or a new perspective or even changed your life. It might be dramatic – torrential rain flooding your marquee meaning you got married in welly boots; or your baby being delivered in the hospital car park. But equally the story might lie in the smallest and most ordinary moments from that day – a look, a word, a thought, a gesture.

8. Your Firsts

You've had a lot of firsts in your life. First memory; first jobs; first kisses; first heartbreaks; first bosses; first friends; first houses; first pay checks; first client; first mistake…

9. Your Worsts

Same topics different adjective – worst memory; worst job; worst kiss; worst heartbreak; worst friends; worst boss; worst houses; worst pay checks; worst clients; worst mistake…

Go back through your calendar or old journals

Those are the main categories to start mining for your stories, but there are so many other places where stories are hidden. Moments that made you laugh and cry; advice taken and advice ignored; family traditions and routines from your past and your present; life-changing conversations. If, like me, you like to journal or keep a diary, flicking back through past volumes can be a rich source of inspiration that might help jog new memories to life. Which events have you recorded, what did you feel about them and how have they influenced you? But if you haven't kept a journal, scroll back through an old appointment diary instead; one or two of the entries may spark an idea.

THE STORYTELLER'S MINDSET

Before I sat down to outline this chapter, I made myself a really strong cuppa. I like my tea strong, but this was stronger than usual, and suddenly the smell of the tannin took me straight back to the tack room at the riding stables where I'd taken lessons as a little girl. The tiniest details suddenly slid back into my head, as though I'd just glimpsed inside a hidden filing drawer I hadn't opened for 30 years. I could see all the bridles hanging from hooks on the wall, the saddles piled and shabby velvet riding hats in a higgledy stack in the corner. I could see the office desk and the open A3-ledger the riding school owner used. And yes, I could smell the smell of that room - strong tea and… of course, ponies.

It's quite likely I have not been in that room since I was around five years old, since that was the age I had started and, rather abruptly, stopped horse riding. My pony, Fudge, had got spooked one day in the riding school and thrown me on to the sandy floor. He was only a Shetland, but that's still a long way to fall when you're three foot nothing. I was so badly shaken that I refused to get back on and, probably relieved to no longer have to pay out for such an expensive hobby, my mother didn't make me go anymore. The next time I went horse riding was 10 years later, when my whole family booked a ride while on holiday in France in the Dordogne. The moment I sat on my horse the fear came flooding back, and I began to shake so badly my parents said I could wait in the car until they came back. It was another 15 years before I rode again. And this time, older and calmer, I actually discovered I loved riding after all, which was sad because I wished I could have been doing it all those previous years.

I hadn't thought about any of those incidents or connected the dots between them until I made that strong cup of tea just before sitting down to write. But here was a story that I could perhaps use one day. There are several potential lessons I can think of that it may fit. But for now, I'll just file it away. Either way, that is what being in the storyteller's mindset is. You look for stories everywhere, you register the ones that come up, and you file them away to use later. This one will be noted down as, *'The time I fell off a horse and refused to ride again.'*

Matching your message to your story

Of course, it's not just about finding a story to tell. You aren't storytelling for pure entertainment, you're telling stories because you have a message to share. Sometimes, as with everyday moment storytelling, the lesson comes to you straight away and you share the story immediately. But other times you have a message you're wanting to convey and you're looking for a story to carry it. This is where you need to match your message to your story and you can do this by doing the following:

1. Decide the message you want to share.
2. Ask yourself: when did you first learn this lesson yourself? Or is there another moment where this lesson felt most potent?
3. Tell the story of the moment you learnt that lesson.

What's the lesson?

What makes a story worth listening to and therefore worth telling? Well, stories traditionally give value. The earliest form of stories, fairytales and fables, were, of course, teaching stories. We taught people lessons by illustrating the consequences of veering off the approved path, taking gifts (or apples) from strangers, or not living in line with societal values. The best stories have lessons, morals and meaning. So the question you need to ask before you share a story is:

- What's the value to my reader?
- What's the lesson?
- What will they come away from this story thinking, feeling or understanding differently?

Matching your story to your audience

Not every story is going to suit every audience, and this is something to really bear in mind. Most of the time you'll be sharing your story with your audience, your soul tribe, your ideal customers, fans and followers. So choosing a story that will resonate with them is going to be easier. But on occasion you may have an opportunity to share your story with a different audience, with a slightly different worldview. In which case, you may create more impact with a different story entirely. For example, what is going to resonate with a room full of women who are mothers juggling parenthood with entrepreneurship, will probably be quite different to a room full of single, career-focused millennials.

SUMMARY

STORYSTORMING – HOW TO MINE FOR STORIES

You have a rich and varied story goldmine, and for every message and lesson you want to share, there is a story from your life that will fit. Sometimes the lesson and value of a story is obvious, other times it's not so obvious – note that story down anyway. It's also important to always consider the audience you're speaking to, and to make sure the story that you're sharing, is right for them.

———

PART THREE
STORY CRAFT

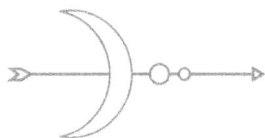

CHAPTER 10
HOW TO TELL A SIMPLE STORY

I F YOU'VE WORKED through Part 2 and followed the Story-Storming exercise in the last chapter, you'll no doubt have plenty of stories you want to start sharing with your audience. But, how do you put it all together? That's exactly what we're going to look at now – how to take your storyline, and craft it into a great story. Let's start by going back to the very basics of story, with a quick review of something all your favourite stories have: the Three-Act structure.

The Three-Act Structure

If you've watched a box-office block buster or read the latest page-turner, in most instances the story will have followed a three-act structure. Just to remind you what that looks like, it goes like this:

There's *A Beginning*
Where you meet a character and a picture is painted of

what life was like before the main events of the story take place (ie the old world).

There's *A Middle*

Where things happen to the character. This is the journey of the story, and includes a transformative moment or event that changes things.

There's *An End*

Where a picture is painted of what life looks like now (the new world) after the events of the story; how things have changed. This is also generally where all the loose ends are tied up so no-one's left feeling cheated.

So that's very simply the structure of a story. Let's dive into the three-act structure with a little more detail now, by starting off with a thrilling tale of daring and adventure... Or maybe just a quick little anecdote about a shopping trip I once had.

Are you sitting comfortably? Then I'll begin...

A couple of years ago, I was Christmas shopping in a big department store, and since I was already loaded up with bags, I decided to take the lift rather than struggle up the escalators. Unfortunately, about 50 other shoppers had thought the exact same thing, and I ended up one cheek squashed against the lift wall, the other crushed up against some random guy who'd considerately kept his empty baby carrier on his back. As I watched every button between the ground and fourth floor light up, I squeezed my phone out of my jeans pocket to pass the journey texting my outrage to my Best Friends' WhatsApp group. Since I'm not a fan of shopping, small spaces, crowds or inconsiderate people, I'm afraid to say there's a good chance I also spent the next 10 minutes passively aggressively sighing every time that blooming baby carrier accidentally jolted my hand.

When the lift finally arrived on the 4th floor, baby-carrier man stepped out of the doors ahead of me and promptly stopped dead, causing me to slam smack bang into the back of him. That was it. I'd had it. What a moron! I thought. Who wears an empty baby carrier on their back in a crowded lift, and then stops dead in front of the lift doors when everyone is trying to get out? And I uttered the most unrestrained and disapproving 'tut' I could muster, just as he turned around with an apologetic smile and said with genuine sincerity, 'Oh, I'm so sorry.'

I don't think the noise I made in response to this kind apology was actually in English, and ironically, now I was the moron stood stock still in front of the lift with irate shoppers pushing to get past me. I opened my mouth a second time to attempt something conciliatory and robustly sane such as, 'That's ok!' or 'Don't worry about it!' Or given the fact that I had still been looking at my phone at point of contact, even, 'Oh, my fault!' But too late. Tom Hardy, yes, THE Tom Hardy, Hollywood actor and my own long-time celebrity crush, was already turning away, and either assuming I had some kind of anger management issue or was about to accost him for a selfie, hurriedly walking off into the sunset (AKA Bentall's toy department), never to be seen again.

Ok so I've told you this story for a couple of reasons. Firstly, because... well, *Tom Hardy*. And secondly, while this is hardly a soul story, more a little personal anecdote (yes, it did actually happen), it has all the basics you need to start your story outline.

CREATING YOUR STORY OUTLINE

> *'I keep six honest serving men (they taught me all I*
>   *knew),*
> *their names are What and Why and When,*
> *and How and Where and Who.'*
> *- Rudyard Kipling*

We're going to use this story example I've just given, to show how you can outline your story using the three-act structure.

The Beginning is all about Context
When did it happen? Where did it happen? And Who did it happen to?

One of the first things your reader wants to do is orientate themselves in space and time, which is why the beginning of a story is all about context. The questions, *'When are we?'* and *'Where are we?'*, are why all fairytales that are generally set in an imaginary place and an imaginary time, start with the words *'Once upon a time in a faraway land.'*

The other thing your audience is going to want to know is *Who is the main character?* A story needs a character for things to happen to, so who is this story happening to? The classic fairytale style would be *'Once upon a time in a land faraway there were a king and queen who desperately longed for a child.'* Or *'a princess who lived with her wicked stepsisters;'* or was *'a poor widow and her son…'*

Your story, however, like the example I've just given, is probably going to be about you; which means *you are the main character.* So, the opening to your story will probably follow a similar structure to mine:

> *'A couple of years ago, I was Christmas shopping in a big department store…'*

The beginning also needs to have something in it that makes the audience want to hear more; a hook if you like, that will grab their interest and make them want to know how it all worked out. A great way to do this is to introduce some kind of problem, conflict or opposition, such as perhaps, an annoying man with an empty baby carrier on his back in a very crowded lift. Or for something to happen that poses a question. For example, perhaps you're really unhappy because you hate your job and dream of travelling the world or starting your own business, but don't think it's ever possible. The question this opens up is, is it possible, and if so, how?

The Middle is where stuff happens
What happened? What was the problem?
What is the conflict?

It's fair to say if nothing happens in your story it's going to be pretty boring. This may seem quite obvious to say, but I have read my fair share of stories in which nothing really happens.

So once you've established the context of your story, move events along and tell them the things that happened next. But here's the key; if what happens next is that everything goes smoothly and totally to plan all the way to the end, you haven't really got a story. For what happened to be in any way interesting, there really needs to be conflict; a predicament that raises the question:

"How is this going to be resolved?"

So this is where ideally what happens next is a bit more opposition or conflict. So for me, it was an annoying person taking up unnecessary space in the lift and generally catching me at an already irritable moment. For the person wanting to leave the corporate career to start a business, it may be actual conflict, such as a bad row with a boss or a spouse. Or maybe the conflict is internal *'How can I ever afford to give up my corporate job and hope to pay my bills?'*

The pivotal moment…

Things don't just need to happen in the middle, they ideally also need to *change*. And that's what a *pivotal moment or twist is for*. A pivotal moment or twist is when Harry Potter finds out he's a wizard; when Marty McFly jumps in the time machine and accidentally heads back thirty years to 1955; when I discover I've unwittingly spent 10 minutes sniffing Tom Hardy's armpit and been totally grumpy and ungrateful about it. The pivotal moment is the thing that happens that changes everything. So taking our corporate-worker story, the pivotal moment may be losing her job, having a health scare that made her totally reassess her priorities, or simply coming up with a fabulous business idea that she's excited enough to go for.

The End is for tying it all up with a lesson learned
What was the outcome? How is the situation or life different?
What's the lesson?

There's nothing more dissatisfying than a story that fizzles out, leaves loose ends or doesn't appear to have a point or a moral. So, the end is for tying it all up into a neat little bow so everyone feels satisfied. Back in the middle of the story, there was a moment that changed everything (the pivotal moment or twist remember?). So this is where we get clear on how life has transformed as a result. Sometimes it will be an actual tangible transformation, like the lady who left her corporate career and now runs a thriving coaching practice helping stressed out career women find more balance in their lives. For others, the transformation may be more a change in perception, seeing something differently or a lesson learned.

You may have noticed with my Tom Hardy story, I didn't actually include the lesson in so many words, it was more implied. But equally, I could have chosen a specific lesson that was suitable for my audience. Perhaps, *'Get your head out of your phone otherwise you'll miss the exciting stuff in life'*. Or maybe even, *'Always be polite – you never know who you're standing next to.'*

Don't forget a CTA…

The end is also where you can include a Call to Action (what you would like your audience or reader to do next). This is usually some kind of invitation, and depending on where, why and to whom you're telling the story, this could be anything from inviting them to book a call with you, check out a website, or just to stay in touch. Or if a 'pitch' isn't appropriate, the Call to Action can simply be the lesson.

SUMMARY

4 STEPS TO OUTLINING A STORY

A simple story outline follows:

    1. Context and character (who, where, when)

    2. A series of events (what, why and the how)

    3. A twist or pivotal moment (this is the transformation element)

    4. The close (the outcome, the lesson, & CTA).

CHAPTER 11

BEGINNINGS, MIDDLES & ENDINGS –TURNING YOUR OUTLINE INTO A GREAT STORY

I N THE LAST chapter, we looked at the basic elements of a story and you learnt how to create a story outline. But now you need to turn that outline into a well-crafted story; one that gets and holds your audience's attention. To do that you need to turn your three-act structure into a compelling opening; a middle that keeps them hooked; and finish up with an ending that leaves them wanting more.

A COMPELLING OPENING

The beginning of your story is in many ways the most important part, because if you don't grab them immediately, you've probably lost your chance. In an ideal world, therefore, you want to capture their interest with your first couple of sentences, or else, before you know it, they'll be scrolling past your post or secretly checking their phone under the table, while you desperately struggle to get your audience back. But once that's happened, they're probably gone for good.

The good news is that whether you're on stage, writing a blog post or an article, the simple fact that you're telling a story is a secret weapon itself, because as you've heard a lot by now, we humans love a story. But what's the difference between a story opening that just becomes background noise, and an opening that gets them to prick up their ears, stop and listen? Well, on top of the hook, which we talked about in the previous chapter, there are a few things to consider.

Start just before everything is about to change.

When you start telling your story, you are setting the stage for what is about to happen, and in order for your audience to fully appreciate the journey and transformation that the story offers, you're probably going to need to paint a picture of what life was like before the main events of the story. This means, you may need to fill in a little of bit of background and do a little bit of scene setting. However, one of the fastest ways for people to lose interest in your story is by starting your story too soon. Nobody wants to listen to a story that takes ages to get going, which means you should start your story at the point just before it's all about to happen. So yes, you can briefly fill in the context: for example, *'I'd been working as a marketing manager for 15 years when…'*, but don't start off with lengthy explanations or long-winded preambles – *start just before the action is about to happen.*

Glennon Doyle does this in the prologue to her memoir *Untamed*.

'Two summers ago, my wife and I took our daughters to the zoo. As we walked the grounds, we saw a sign advertising the park's big event: the Cheetah Run…'

The book begins with Glennon taking her kids to the zoo where they see a cheetah who's been trained to chase a toy bunny. Notice, she starts just as the action is about to happen, not with her saying that morning, *'Shall we go to the zoo?'* followed by them getting into the car and driving there, buying their tickets etc. She also starts with context – *who, when, where?* And once that's established, they immediately see a sign for the park's big event, where the main action of the story takes place: The Cheetah Run.

The opening also feels relatable, personal and normal, and yet there is still this blistering sense that it's about to deliver a very profound lesson, which it does. So remember again, your stories don't have to be dramatic; trust that the story is enough.

Don't be tempted by click-bait openings

Another way people try to spice their story up a bit, or try to lure people in, is with a sensational statement such as, *'I thought I was going to die'*, or *'It was the worst moment of my life'*. These things might work in the short term on social-media platforms, but ultimately, it feels click-baity, a little clumsy, and unoriginal. You can, of course, use an intriguing opener that seeds a promise of the kind of story you're about to tell, but for that to work it has to feel different and it has to feel fresh, and it must not feel like a cheap trick to grab someone's attention.

Lisa Lister's book *Witch* doesn't start dramatically. It simply begins at the moment she felt compelled to write a book about what it means to be a witch in the 21st Century. It also happens to follow a classic founding story format. Returning to the questions we used in Chapter 6 to pull together the elements that make up your founder's story, here's how they fit with Lisa's opening.

When did she have the idea to write the book?
She was sitting in a café in LA with friends.

What were the series of events that led to the idea?
A conversation they had. In fact, it's the account of that conversation, (when it happened, where it took place, who the characters were and what happened next) that opens the book:

> 'February 16th. I'm sitting in café Gratitude, Venice Beach with Dana Gillespie and Holly Grigg-Spall. The three of us are joking we are the Holy Freakin' trinity of modern day witches…'

Brené Brown starts her Ted Talk about *The Power of Vulnerability* with a very simple anecdote. She says:

> 'A couple of years ago an event planner called me because I was going to do a speaking event, and she called and said "I'm really struggling with how to write about you on the little flyer…"'

The event planner goes on to explain that she's concerned that if she describes Brené as a 'researcher' no one will come to the talk, so instead she's decided to call her a 'storyteller'. It turns out this was the conversation that made Brené realise that yes indeed, she is a storyteller, and this is the transformation and shift of perception in her story. But this opening also serves as a neat way to introduce herself in a conversational, engaging and self-effacing way, while alleviating any pre-conception that she is little more than just a boring researcher.

THE TRICKY MIDDLE (KEEPING 'EM HOOKED)

What is it that hooks us on a story and keeps us watching, reading or listening all the way through the middle to the end? The characters? The setting? The subject? Yes, these things can definitely be a draw. But the one thing that really makes you want to listen to a story and not get distracted and forget about it, is conflict. We talked about this a little bit in the last chapter, but let's look a little more closely at what conflict is in a story and how to use it.

Conflict is when two strong opposing forces go up against each other making the outcome of a story uncertain. You may think of conflict and automatically think of physical conflict. Of course, *'who's going to win the fight?'* can be a compelling question, but more often than not, the types of conflict you'll be using in your own personal stories, will be a more subtle psychological or emotional kind of struggle.

> Conflict is when two strong opposing forces go up against each other making the outcome of a story uncertain.

Things such as, success versus failure, life versus death, freedom versus oppression, hate versus forgiveness. When you introduce this conflict it makes the outcome uncertain which gets us asking *'How's it all going to end?'* If there isn't any conflict, there isn't any question mark, and it won't hold your attention. Imagine a *Game of Thrones* with no one partic-ularly fussed over who becomes King? Or a *Mrs Doubtfire* where the divorce was amicable? Or a *Pride and Prejudice* where Lizzy and Mr Darcy tell each other they love each other from the off and are married within a month.

Without conflict, without the *'Will they, won't they?'* question, there is no compulsion to carry on. Conflict, however, stirs emotions and makes it hard for us to look away. It asks a question that we as humans find it difficult to leave unanswered. Was leaving your well-paid corporate job to become a small holder actually going to make you happier? Would you ever be free of that abusive partner and would they ever get their comeuppance? Can a woman run a successful business *and* be a good and present mother?

HOW TO FINISH

The best way to end a story is to leave them wanting more. This means that one of the most powerful pieces of advice for how to finish a story on a high, is to tell your story and then stop! This may sound pretty obvious, but when you're not used to telling a story, there can be a tendency to tell it, then explain why you've told it, and then just to be sure, tell them what you want them to think about this and that and oh, that as well…. This is a sure-fire way to ruin the magic you've so carefully crafted. Which means the story is not only enough, but you don't need to justify why you've told it.

There are a couple of other things to think about to make your ending truly pack a punch:

1. *Get clear on the teaching moment or lesson*

A good story has got to give value. Sometimes the story is helping people understand who you are and where you come from (your Founder's Story), but often the value in a story is that you're using a teaching moment. Going back to Glennon Doyle's cheetah story, she closes on the lesson that puts the entire story into the context of what her book is about. She imagines what the cheetah is thinking as she watches her stalk around her small enclosure. She imagines that perhaps the cheetah is craving something more like *'ink-black skies,'* *'wide open savannahs…'* She imagines that the cheetah sighs and tells herself that she's got a good enough life and is crazy to *'long for what doesn't exist.'*

And then Glennon closes on the lesson:

'Tabitha. You are not crazy. You are a goddamn cheetah.'

Glennon does not spoon-feed the lesson. She trusts the story is enough and it's the hook for the rest of the book. If she was telling this story in a talk, however, she may then go on and perhaps be a little more explicit in explaining the lesson, as you will see from the Steve Jobs and Marianne Cantwell examples that follow.

2. Carry the Flame

There are two types of story; one where a character goes on a journey, doesn't learn any lessons at all and has a sticky ending (more commonly known as a tragedy in literature). The other type of story is one where the character goes on a journey, some pretty shady things may or may not happen to them, they learn a lesson, grow as a person, and it all ends on a positive note. The truth is, your audience is going to feel more inclined to want to hear what you say if what you say leaves them feeling uplifted. Which is why people like stories that are positive. It doesn't mean they can't deal with heavy stuff, but it's so much easier to deal with the heavy stuff if the overall message is one of hope. So if you're sharing something dark, what is the light that you're sharing? What is the hope that you're passing on? What is the lesson? End your story with a feeling of hope and carry the flame.

3. Come Full Circle

Really great stories seed the end at the beginning. This is what gives it a sense of completion. I'll give you an example of this from Steve Jobs who was not only a genius and entrepreneur, but also a great storyteller. If you check out his commencement speech at Stanford, you'll see that he tells three stories. And the first one about 'connecting the dots', seeds the end in the beginning beautifully. He starts off explaining that he is a college drop-out, and that in fact the closest he ever got to a commencement ceremony was standing there giving that commencement speech that day. He goes on to talk about the journey he went on as a college drop-out and how it actually led to great success. He closes the story with this:

'You can't connect the dots looking forwards, you can only connect them looking backwards. So, you have to trust the dots will somehow connect in your future... Because believing that the dots will connect down the road, will give you the confidence to follow your heart, even when it leads you off the well-worn path. And that will make all the difference.'

Steve brings his story full circle, and shows that although dropping out of college didn't make sense at the time, it does now. He ends with a lesson, a moral – he is hopeful and he doesn't labour the point. He tells the story. He sums it up with a simple lesson, and he leaves it at that.

· · ·

Marianne Cantwell also brings her story full circle in her Ted Talk entitled, *The Hidden Power of not (always) Fitting In.* She starts off with an anecdote about how her teacher had once pulled her aside, and explained that they both have one thing in common – they are both generalists. Marianne then goes on to explain how she later discovered there was another way to see being a generalist – something which had very limiting and negative connotations – which was instead, seeing it as 'living liminally', something her talk demonstrates, is far more inspiring and positive.

Here's how she closes her story:

> *'…. Imagine, if my teacher when I was 16, had known about what we'd talked about here today. Here is what he might have said: "Marianne, you and I have something in common: We are liminal. And the world won't always understand that. But I want you to know it's a valuable way to be. And don't just take my word for it. The examples are all around when you know how to look. So, don't hide that away. You see, you won't succeed despite your liminality, but because of it."'*

Marianne brings the tale full circle, the story is complete and the question she raised at the beginning, 'Was being a generalist something that holds you back or makes you thrive?', has its answer.

SUMMARY

BEGINNINGS, MIDDLES & ENDS

Compelling Openings

- Start from the moment things change.
- Trust that the story is enough. The most poignant stories are often the least glamorous or dramatic.

Keeping them hooked

- What conflict that makes the outcome uncertain?
- What is the question that will keep them going until the end?

A Powerful Ending

- Tell your story and then stop
- Get clear on the teaching moment
- Carry the flame (and the hope)
- Come full circle

CHAPTER 12

BUILDING THE WORLD OF YOUR STORY

T HE BEST STORIES LEAVE A TRACE. To this day, I can vividly conjure moments from my grandmother's life in the 1920s, 30s and 40s, as though I'd seen it all in a movie. My Nan, aged 4 or 5, sitting on the street kerb using a pin to prick out the seeds of a pomegranate her grandad had bought her as a treat; in her mid-teens, dressing gown clutched around her standing in Bryanston Square during one of the worst night raids of The Blitz, watching the fires blaze over London; aged 16, at the London Astoria on Charing Cross Road, and the way her favourite red dress swung out about her hips as she danced to the band music in the middle of the afternoon.

Story isn't a passive experience, it's a co-creative one. So, I don't remember which of those details my nan told me, and which ones were gaps that I created myself in my imagination. We all do this to a certain extent, we hear a story and conjure the images in our minds, filling in details that the storyteller didn't paint. The more skilfully you can tell a story, therefore, the more rich and vibrant those images become in your audience's mind, and the more likely they are to remember your story. They might not be able to remember the exact words that you used, or what the characters said, but they'll remember impressions, moods, emotions, sometimes even colours, smells and textures, because your storytelling will have helped to have created a movie in their mind. There are four simple ways you can enrich your storytelling to help your audience do this.

HOW TO CREATE A MOVIE IN THEIR MIND

1. *Remember how it looked, felt, sounded*

'I take that goddamn scrunchie out of my greasy hair. I get out of those stale pyjamas and take a shower. I shave - not my beard, but at least my legs. I put on some decent clothes. I brush my teeth, I wash my face. I put on a lipstick - and I never wear lipstick. I clear my desk of its clutter, throw open a window, and maybe even light a scented candle. I might even put on perfume for God's sake.'

ELIZABETH GILBERT, BIG MAGIC

In this excerpt from Elizabeth Gilbert's book Big Magic, she makes her story a sensory experience and you should too. Thinking about all five of your senses when you tell a story, helps you to create a world that feels so much more tangible to your audience. When you're starting to tell a story, ask yourself,

What can you see?
    (Not just objects and things, but textures, and light and colours)
    What can you hear?
    What can you smell?
    What can you taste?
    *What can you feel? (*Not just in terms of touch, but emotions, too).

. . .

You don't need to describe every single sense all the time, because the truth is we aren't aware of every single sense at every single moment - if we were, that would be totally overwhelming. There are usually one or two senses that will be dominant during a particular moment or story. In the Big Magic example, there's an emphasis towards touch/feeling and smell, with adjectives such as 'greasy', 'stale,' and the action of throwing open the windows and lighting scented candles. Work out what the dominant senses are for your story, and use this detail to help your audience build the world of your story.

2. Describe how they drink their coffee

We've all heard someone tell a lie and perhaps been alerted to the fact by the vagueness of the detail in the story we're being told. That's why when we use specific detail in a story it makes our audience think, '*Yes, this feels true.*' From the kid who won't eat their toast if it's cut into triangles; to the man who drinks his coffee black with a teaspoon of butter; to the specific type of flowers on the table, or breed of dog tied to the fence.

Specific detail makes your story feel like it's rooted in real life and brings two dimensional people, places and things into the 3D. Specific detail can also anchor your story in a particular era or location; or even be used to build rapport with your audience with reference to familiar cultural nuances, such as the exact brand of biscuits everyone's grandmother had in their cupboards in the 90s, or the TV show they all loved to watch on a Friday night after school. In fact, the more granular you can get with the detail, the more truthful your story will feel.

Let's look at another extract from Steve Jobs' Stanford commencement speech.

> *'I returned Coke bottles for the 5c deposit to buy food with, and I would walk the seven miles across town every Sunday night to get one good meal a week at the Hare Krishna Temple.'*

There are lots of specific detail in this one sentence; the specific brand of bottles he returned; the specific amount of money he received for them; he didn't just 'walk across town' for his dinner, he walked *'seven miles'* across it. This is also a good example of another important storytelling technique that you'll probably remember from your school days, but is so important to use…

3. Show don't tell

Telling your reader what something was like is nowhere near as powerful as showing them. In the previous extract, Steve Jobs didn't just tell his audience that he was stony broke, he showed them he was by explaining the different ways he tried to make some extra cash, and how he fed himself week-to-week. When you're telling a story, beware of just relaying what happened or how things were, and look for ways to paint a picture so your audience can really understand what you mean; don't just tell them how sick you were, for example, show them how sick you were by describing how you had to get your neighbour to take the kids to school for you, or how you couldn't walk up the stairs in your house without taking a break half way up.

4. Use dialogue

Using actual dialogue (*'I'm leaving you,'* she said) rather than relaying what that person said, (*'then she told me she was leaving me'*), is not only a more succinct way to tell your story, but the fastest way to bring your audience directly into a scene. It doesn't mean you can't ever narrate any elements of a conversation – sometimes this is useful when you're trying to move the story along to a pivotal moment, but if the conversation itself is important, narrating it rather than using direct speech can dampen the impact. In Brené Brown's *The Call to Courage* talk available on Netflix, she uses dialogue to tell part of the story of a time she and her husband went open water swimming. She says,

> *'All of a sudden I catch Steve's eye and I say, "Steve,"*
> *And he says "Yeah?"*
> *"I feel so connected to you right now, I'm so glad that we're spending this time together doing this."*
> *And he looks back at me and he goes, "Yeah, water's good!" and he keeps swimming.'*

If she had *narrated* what they said to each other, in contrast, it would perhaps have sounded something like this:

> *'I catch Steve's eye and I tell him that I feel so connected to him, and how I am so glad that we are spending that time together; and he just looks at me and says "the water's good" and carries on swimming.'*

If you look at these two examples of the same story, hopefully you can see that when you narrate a conversation rather than using dialogue, you (the storyteller) get in between your listener and the scene. This means that the person hearing the story is one person removed from the action, which makes it harder for them to become immersed in the story. For important moments, therefore, use the exact words someone says in dialogue to make it easier for your audience to suspend reality and enter into the world of your story.

. . .

5. Breathe life into your characters

Good storytellers help you to create a strong mental image of the people (ie characters) in the stories they are telling. I can clearly see in my mind's eye the people my grandmother talked about from her past: her beautiful friend Peggy Wilson with her full red lipsticked-mouth and finger curls, who was far too aloof to ever be walked home by a boy. Or the first time my Nan saw my Grandad walking down the Edgware Road in his naval uniform, with his long loping gait, and how his cap was pushed slightly back on his head all the better to see his black hair and blue eyes. Or Mrs Noble, the wife of a writer she worked for; she was an actress who was never seen eating a single morsel of food. Or another wealthy lady my great grandmother worked for, who would flounce around her town house all day, wearing a silk Chinese dressing gown and carrying a cigarette holder in her hand.

Whenever there's a character in your story, find a detail or two to help bring them to life. How much you include will depend on how long the story you're telling is, and how important that person (character) is to the story. In Malcolm Gladwell's Ted Talk *Choice, Happiness and Spaghetti Sauce*, he tells a story about a friend of his called Howard, and because Howard is essentially the main character of the talk, Gladwell takes quite some time for us to paint a mental image of what Howard is like. He says:

> 'Howard is about this high and he's round and he's in his 60s. He has big huge glasses and thinning grey hair, and he has a kind of wonderful exuberance and vitality. He has a parrot, and he loves the opera, and he is a great aficionado of mediaeval history. By profession he's a psychophysicist.'

. . .

Gladwell tells us what Howard looks like (his height, his shape, his hair), and he gives us a feel for who Howard is. In fact, he shows us who he is rather than tells us. So rather than explaining he's got lots of diverse interests and is perhaps a little eccentric, he instead gives concrete examples; Howard owns a parrot, he likes the opera and mediaeval history, and he's also a scientist.

The other thing to bear in mind when bringing your characters to life is to make this relative to the person's role in the story. If they are the main character, like Howard was here, they may warrant a couple of sentences or more. If they are someone you just meet in passing, you may just put them into context: 'my friend from work' or 'my next-door neighbour'; or if they are a minor but slightly more significant character, you may include a tiny detail to help build a mental image. Here's one I once used when telling a story that mentioned an old friend who was, *'a scatty eco-warrior from Dorset, who once came to work in her pyjama top because she'd 'forgotten to put a wash on'.*

SUMMARY

BUILDING THE WORLD OF YOUR STORY

Like a movie that plays in your audience's minds, the more
richly and vibrantly you paint the picture of the world of
your story, the more realistic it will feel, and the
more memorable it will be.

———

CHAPTER 13
DEEPENING YOUR MESSAGE

GOOD STORY ISN'T simply the sum of its parts – it's not just about working out the beginning, the middle, the end, painting a few pictures with words and offering up a lesson. The best stories have a deeper meaning that goes beyond the things that happen and the words that are said; they hold a universal truth that shows that our lives and experiences can look entirely different on the surface, but that on the inside we're all the same. This is what we call 'the story behind the story', and it's the deeper message behind your soul story.

THE STORY BEHIND THE STORY

As a journalist, finding 'the story behind the story' was really what my job was about. People would come to me because they wanted me to write a feature on how they had started their business, and so when we'd have our initial chat on the phone to see if they had a story I could tell, the first thing they'd do was to tell me their 'founder's story'. Which some-times, was very interesting. But, I always knew that most often, the part of their story that was *really* interesting, the bit that was going to get people attracted to their business or their work, was the bit they didn't think of telling me straight away because they thought it was irrelevant or boring or too personal for anyone to care about. When really it's the stories that people can't find on google that are really going to get people engaged with you and your business.

Because, as you know, what's personal is universal. So often, other people's stories are how we make sense of our own hopes, dreams and challenges. My job as a features writer, therefore, was to ask the right questions and to listen for the little clues and breadcrumbs that would help me uncover the real story. In fact, the most common question I needed to keep asking was simply *'why?'*

"Why did you start your business?"
   "But why did you leave your job?"
   "And why did you feel undervalued or trapped or lost?"
   "And why was this your calling?"

Because as the 5 whys exercise in chapter 6 shows, when we keep asking why, we are able to quickly boil down the complex web of our lives and thoughts and choices, into a simple relatable truth.

The Desire to Belong

One Spring, a few years ago, I travelled to a small rehearsal hall in Stroud to interview the, now late, Nell Gifford; a talented horsewoman and ringmaster of her very own travelling circus. On the surface, the founding story of Gifford's Circus was that Nell had run away with the circus on a gap year when she was 18, and having fallen in love with the way of life, she decided to bring the village-green-style circus back to the UK. It sounded fun and glamorous, but an unlikely path for a young woman who'd read English at Oxford, so of course the first question my story had to pursue was *Why?*

I already knew that when Nell was a teenager, her mother had been brain damaged in a riding accident, and when our conversation reached this point, she told me how her family home had been broken up. She said, *'Family life was over in a day.'* That had been when she had joined the circus, and not only fell in love with the people and the lifestyle, but found the sense of home and belonging she had lost. That, for me was the story behind the story. Not everyone reading about Nell's experiences could relate to her dream or her lifestyle, or even to losing a parent so young, but everyone can understand that longing to find your place in the world; your people and where you belong.

The need to give back

Around a similar time, I was asked to write a feature on Lizzie Carr, a green activist who had paddle-boarded the length of the UK to raise awareness of plastic pollution. She'd been featured in the newspapers a few times, but there was very little personal information in those articles, and so before our conversation, I didn't really understand what had motivated Lizzie to do what she did. It was, of course, impressive and admirable; but on trawling through the small number of news reports on this feat, I found no indication of why she felt so compelled to devote so much of her time and energy to doing this. Surely there were easier ways to raise awareness?

We met in Lizzie's South London home, and over a cup of tea we talked about how much she cared about the environment and how it had been paddle-boarding on the Thames which had opened her eyes to just how much pollution there was on our river ways. Ok, this made sense, but *why not donate to a local charity or join a local beach clean?* This is when, rather hesitantly at first, Lizzie explained to me her 'why'.

In her early twenties, as a young, carefree marketing executive, with a love of travelling and a boyfriend she hoped to spend her life with, she'd been diagnosed with stage 4 cancer. It had been getting out into nature on her paddle board which had helped Lizzie heal emotionally. Against all odds, Lizzie was now in remission, and she explained to me that she wanted to spend the life she'd nearly lost helping to heal the natural world that had been such an important part of her recovery – she was motivated by a desire to 'give back'.

The Journey to Heal

In 2014, my cousin Ben Harris asked me to help him with a book he'd written and been sitting on for nearly 10 years; it was a travel memoir that charted several months of a journey he had taken, largely alone and on foot, when he was just 19 years old. It was a journey of absolutely epic proportions, an odyssey really which took him through Thailand, China, Tibet, Nepal, India and even Afghanistan. I, of course, had always known he had done this – he'd send my Dad occasional email updates charting his travels, which he had absolutely loved receiving, and would forward on to me (and no doubt others, too).

But it wasn't until I actually looked at the manuscript, that I realised I hadn't really ever considered why he had done it? I was only a few years older than him, and while I can hardly call myself the adventurous type, I couldn't quite conceive what would inspire someone to so doggedly pursue such a long and gruelling journey with never an SOS call home? I don't think he once caught a plane, and there were even times when he was taken seriously ill, got lost, was injured, became severely dehydrated, was attacked (once by wild dogs, on other occasions by desperate humans), was frozen to the bone, scared and had nowhere safe to sleep for the night – surely most 19 year olds would have phoned home for a plane ticket quicker than you could order a Big Mac with cheese?

But the answer lay in the very first chapter Ben had written – he'd called it 'The Wave'. Because something I had also known but never really joined the dots on, was that at 19, Ben had been a dive instructor in Thailand, just as the Boxing Day tsunami had hit. He'd been lucky. Diving behind one of the islands at the time of landfall he'd been protected from the worst of the wave, and had later been rescued from the sea by a Navy ship. But when he returned to land he found the life he had built in ruin, and friends and acquaintances who'd been staples of his every day, had just been swept away. Over the next few weeks, he stayed and helped with the recovery and clean-up efforts, during which time he witnessed countless terrible scenes.

Since he now lives on an island in Panama, we worked together on the book chatting over email, on the phone, and once spent a day together in person writing and editing on one of his trips home. It was then that he explained to me, that after all he had witnessed, of course he wanted to go home. But he had to do it in a way that wouldn't anger – well, he wasn't sure what? The Gods? Mother Nature?

And there was something else. Because as I worked with him through each chapter, each experience, story and beat, the one thing that became so apparent to me was this: while he was living on his wits, getting sick, sometimes, scared, injured or lost, he was also passing through community after community and culture after culture, where he was also helped, welcomed, amazed, educated, inspired, informed, and ultimately helped on the path to healing by the people he met, by the earth he walked upon, and the nature he walked through.

This was a young man who had witnessed so much horror

in the tsunami; a teenager who was grieving for friends, a human who had witnessed death and destruction. I got it. How *did* you return home to friends and family and a world that had absolutely no idea of what any of that meant? Ben's was not just a story about an adventurous teenager with wanderlust who had travelled halfway across the world on foot; it was the story of how we process and move forwards with the grief and trauma of things that are too painful to accept. The Detour, by my cousin Ben Harris, is available to buy on Amazon at https://amzn.to/41xcD9V.

Story is about transformation

Transformation is at the heart of every good story, and it's often the thing that triggers that transformation which helps us to work out the story behind our story. So often, stories start with some kind of unexpected change. Following our three-act structure, we begin by painting the picture of what life was like, then something happens to change it all, and we set off on a journey that finishes in a new life situation, a new world, or even a new mindset or perspective.

The reason I left my job in magazines, became an entrepreneur and began working and writing for myself, was because my dad had died aged 63 leaving his novel half written; for Nell it was her family life being destroyed by her mother's accident; for Lizzie it was a health diagnosis; for Ben it was surviving a tragedy. Your pivotal moment may not be so dramatic; it might be losing a job, a relationship ending, it might even be a situation, moment or a conversation that suddenly made you see the truth of things. It doesn't matter. Sometimes it will be a phoenix moment where everything just burns to the ground and you rise from the ashes; other times that pivotal moment is literally a pivot, you're spun around by fate, and suddenly find yourself facing an entirely new direction.

. . .

But there will be a moment that led to your transformation, and it's always personal – that is the story behind the story.

The Telling Detail

My grandmother loved her grandad, Bill. He must have been a very old grandfather, as the only picture I can remember seeing of him is of my Nan as a very small toddler in a white pinafore, and him a stooping, white haired old man in a well-worn suit. While my Nan was born in London just off the Edgware Road and was street-smart and sassy, a girl who was in constant trouble and mischief; Bill was a gentle old country boy, who'd come to London to find work and then later sent for his family.

I always feel incredibly sad when I think about Bill, even though I've never heard many stories about him really, mainly sketchy glimpses of who he might have been: how he had no teeth and could only eat bread that had been soaked in milk or water; that he hated London and only hadn't returned to the Suffolk countryside because his wife had refused to move back; that he lived out the last few years of his very hard life in a couple of rooms that overlooked an old workhouse.

One story I do know though is this. My Nan, who like everyone else he called Cis, was going through some sort of teenaged drama about a friend or a boy or a job; and she'd flumped down on to a chair in her mother's kitchen (where her grandad had perhaps been sitting supping his milk-soaked bread), and she'd dramatically announced, *'Oh I just want to die!'* To which old Bill had replied, no doubt in his soft lilting Suffolk tones, perhaps gently placing an arthritic and work-gnarled hand upon hers, *'You'll find it is very hard to die.'*

That story has always given me a knot of sadness in my

stomach. Because with that one sentence I wonder what he meant; I imagine how he must have felt in those last years of his life. When my Nan told me that story, she didn't have to tell me, *'Oh, my grandad was old and tired, and life held no softness for him;'* she didn't have to tell me that every night he closed his eyes on the cot where he slept, and wasn't scared of death, but invited it. That story was there in those seven words. *'…it can be very hard to die.'* That was the detail that spoke a thousand words; the telling detail, the one detail that is the key to someone's story.

So, the telling detail is what I always hope to find when I'm telling a story. It doesn't have to be something someone says; it can be an image, a phrase, a moment, a look, a possession, even an empty space. The telling detail is the thing that sums up a story or a scene or a moment, or a place, or a person, beautifully. In the larger context of the story though, the telling detail puts everything that came before it into context and shines a light on that one message the story is trying to share. It's the essence of the story. So often it can be a very ordinary and simple thing. For example, in one of my favourite songs, *Diorama by BellX1* which is about a mother whose children have grown up and moved away, the telling detail is the bed made up in the spare room that's never slept in; the telling detail is often a simple everyday detail that throws the story into a whole new light.

Finding the telling detail

Working out the telling detail in your story is about not trying too hard, and trusting it will make itself known. Sometimes it will already be there and you won't have noticed so don't push it – it'll come if it's meant to. One way to work it out though is to ask yourself, *What is the one message this story is trying to impart?* Then look for the detail that portrays this truth: the moment, image, detail or phrase, that's worth a thousand words. Then, once you find it, don't explain it, don't justify it, don't tell people what you want them to think it means; just choose the detail that holds the essence of your story, and let it speak for itself.

One of my favourite quotes is from Rumi, a 13th Century Persian poet who said,

> 'You are not a drop in the ocean;
> You are the entire ocean in a drop.'

And that's kind of how I feel about the telling detail. It's not just a moment in the story, a detail about someone you meet, or something somebody says; the telling detail is the whole story in a single moment.

YOUR STORY IS BIGGER THAN YOU

A FINAL NOTE FROM ME

It was 2021 when I first had the idea to create *Soul Story*, which was first a course, and later became this book. I've always loved stories and storytelling, but up until that point consuming stories had been about entertainment and inspiration, and in my work I was teaching it purely as a communication tool for business (which, of course, it's great for and this book has hopefully shown you how). But one afternoon as I sat working in my bedroom, the kids making a racket downstairs playing Dino Bingo with their Dad, I had a sudden download, or moment of clarity, of just how powerful story really is. And I had an almost tangible vision of how every story that is told adds to the collective harmony of the universe, and how it is that harmony, a bit like the soundtrack to a movie, which sets the tone, and emotions and feelings of the world that we live in.

At the time, the world that I and everybody else was living in had a lot going on, and as you read this, no doubt there still is. And knowing that old adage, *'whoever tells the best stories has the stage'*, I felt frustrated. Because so often I've observed that the players who easily find themselves centre stage, and who have no trouble getting their voices heard, are not necessarily those always acting with the best interests of the individual or the collective at heart.

There is no better story, no truer story than a person's lived experience, and I had this sudden desire to counter this and to help more ordinary people to use their platforms to make an impact sharing what they have seen and heard and witnessed with their own eyes and ears and heart; to share their soul stories and speak their truth into the world.

I imagined what would happen if there were more stories going into the collective from everyday people like you and me; from purpose-driven entrepreneurs, change-makers, people who are here to help and to heal; people who want to live abundantly and give abundantly, and share their stories in a conscious way. I imagined what would happen to the collective harmony of the world if that was the case. What would that new soundtrack be?

Imagine…

And perhaps, like John Lennon, *I'm* just a dreamer, but I realised I could do nothing with this notion; or I could do something. I chose to do something, and decided that if all I did with my work, was to help 1,000 heart-led people become 1,000 storytellers, that would make a difference. Because 1,000 storytellers could surely touch millions of lives.

And that's why I wrote this book.

So, my hope is that *Soul Story* has not only inspired you, but empowered you, and helped you to realise that you not only have stories to tell, but you have reasons big and small to tell them. Perhaps you know others who need this book, and if you do, I hope you will share it with them. Because if just you and 999 others become storytellers and start to share your soul story, your truth, with the world; well, I can't quite imagine what that new collective harmony might start to sound or feel like. But I do know it can only be more beautiful. Because it will be ringing with truth, and with love.

Cate

ABOUT THE AUTHOR

Cate Butler Ross is a writer & book mentor, working with successful coaches, experts and thought leaders who want to write *the* book that will blow up their business – and create the book funnel to go with it. Cate also runs The Luminous Press, through which she offers a range of author services provided by a trusted network of publishing professionals, including ghostwriting and copy-editing, through to full production packages.

Cate began her career in UK national magazines back in 2002 as a features writer, and went on to commission and edit for titles including Woman & Home and Country Living Magazine. She has written for many other popular titles including *Woman*, *Prima* and *The Simple Things*, and has interviewed, profiled and told the stories of hundreds of celebrities, industry leaders, Olympians and thought leaders, from Sharon Osbourne and Trudi Styler, Jo Malone and Karren Brady, to Roger Moore and David Attenborough.

If you want to explore different ways of working privately with Cate, email us at hello@theluminous.media.

Check out Cate's latest offers and freebies at www.thelumi nous.media/quick-links/

📕 📷

WORK WITH ME

PRIVATE & GROUP BOOK COACHING

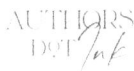

AUTHORS DOT Ink

AUTHORS DOT INK

The 9-month group book coaching program for established coaches, experts and thought leaders ready to turn their expertise into a book that will blow up your business.

https://theluminous.media/program/

PRIVATE BOOK COACHING

If you prefer to work 1:1, Cate also offers a limited number of private book coaching packages. Each one is bespoke, and tailored to your specific needs. If you'd like to discuss how this could work for you email Cate at hello@theluminous.media

THE LUMINOUS PRESS
WRITING & PUBLISHING SUPPORT FOR BUSINESS OWNERS

THE LUMINOUS

YOUR BESPOKE AUTHOR DREAM TEAM

You not only want to write a book that's going to sky-rocket your authority and set you apart as the obvious choice in your field, but you want to write *the book* that's going to blow up your business.

And if you're serious about self-publishing, you need a publishing partner who knows what it takes for a book to stand out against the bestsellers. At The Luminous Press we pull together your very own, bespoke publishing dream team that will help you write, publish and set your book up for success.

With experts ranging from book coaches, ghostwriters, copyeditors and designers, right through to digital marketing experts who'll design and create your book funnel for you, our authors can do as much, or as little as they desire for their book project, safe in the knowledge their book will be in the hands of their dream clients and customers within 6-12 months.

Find out more about our latest packages at www.thelumi nous.media/publish

BIBLIOGRAPHY AND VIDEO REFERENCES

BOOKS

Witch: Unleashed. Untamed. Unapologetic, By Lisa Lister; Hay House; https://www.hayhouse.com/witch-paperback

Untamed: Stop Pleasing, Start Living, by Glennon Doyle; Vermilion; https://www.penguin.co.uk/books/441930/untamed-by-glennon-doyle/9781785043352

Big Magic, by Elizabeth Gilbert; Bloomsbury; https://www.bloomsbury.com/uk/big-magic-9781408866764/

Daring Greatly, by Brené Brown; https://brenebrown.com/book/daring-greatly/

TALKS

Brené Brown; The Power of Vulnerability; Ted Talk; https://www.ted.com/talks/brene_brown_the_power_of_vulnerability/c

Steve Jobs; Stanford Commencement Speech; https://news.stanford.edu/2005/06/12/youve-got-find-love-jobs-says/

Marianne Cantwell; The Hidden Power of Not (Always) Fitting in; Ted Talk; https://mariannecantwell.com/tedtalk/

Malcolm Gladwell; Choice, Happiness and Spaghetti Sauce; Ted Talk; https://www.ted.com/talks/malcolm_gladwell_choice_happiness_and_spaghetti_sauce

Brené Brown; The Call to Courage; Netflix

ACKNOWLEDGEMENTS

Thank you to everyone who has inspired and supported *Soul Story*: to my husband, Will, who's always wisely understood that a happy wife is one who writes, and has always supported my dream; to my Nanny, Cis, who showed me the power and importance of sharing our personal histories and experience; to my darling Dad, who always believed I'd be an author – I only wish you were here to tell; to my Mum, my (very bias) first reader and cheerleader; to Charlie and Ross, who are more than just my siblings, but my creative sparring partners in work and in life; without you all, nothing would seem possible, and everything would be far too ordinary. And this book would never have been finished.

I'm very grateful to the incredible writers, storytellers, and speakers, whose skill and technique has long inspired mean, and which I've been able to use as teaching examples in this book. Finally, to everyone who has ever supported my work, as a client, customer, listener, reader, or subscriber – thank you for helping me realise I knew something that was worth sharing.

THE LUMINOUS PRESS

Printed in Great Britain
by Amazon

29968596R00091